This book was writt(
150th anniversary (
arriving in the City

October !

1850 - 2000

The book is in two parts

Part 1: A brief history of Shrub Hill station and local area, memories from some staff.
By John Boynton.

Part 2: A list of significant dates for railways of Worcester.
By Stephen Widdowson.

Steam Loco No. 1639 is seen on the Vinegar branch, crossing through the Midland Red bus depot, at Padmore Street Crossing. The driver of the loco is Ken Mathews. 1963. *(Photo: Howard Griffiths)*

Worcester 150

Copyright © 2000

Worcester 150, John Boynton and Stephen Widdowson

ISBN No. 0 9522248 8 7

FRONT COVER

Top: *A rare photo of Shrub Hill station still with the overall roof, however it is showing signs that it many not be on much longer. A LMS Black 5 stands on platform 5, with a service to the west, while a GWR 'Star' class can be seen on one of the middle roads, 7th August 1935.*

(Photo: Jack Saunders Collection)

Bottom: *150132 is seen on 28th July 2000, in this picture taken from the same place as the one above.*

(Photo: Stephen Widdowson)

BACK COVER

Top: *'Stowe Grange' No. 6856, is seen at the north end of Shrub Hill on 4th April 1965.*

(Photo: Roy Godfrey)

Bottom: *Central Trains new class 170 unit No. 170517, is seen stabled on the middle road at Shrub Hill.*

(Photo: Stephen Widdowson)

WORCESTER 150

One Hundred and Fifty Years of Railways in the City : 1850-2000

Prologue : The Arrival of the Railway : The Line to Hereford
Branches & Works : Train Services : Tales of Shrub Hill

PROLOGUE

Worcester Shrub Hill saw its first passenger train on 5th October 1850, although the city had featured in railway time-tables for some years before that. Today's high speed main line between Birmingham and Bristol passes to the east of the city. The Birmingham & Gloucester Railway (B&G) opened that line in 1840, although the final two miles, into the London & Birmingham Railway's terminus at Birmingham Curzon Street, were not opened until August 1841. The B&G's headquarters were at Bromsgrove, at the foot of the Lickey Incline. With a gradient of 1:37 and a length of almost two miles up to Blackwell, this was - and remains - a unique stretch of line, exceptionally difficult to work in the days of steam. The incline, together with the stations at Blackwell and Barnt Green, opened in September 1840. Barnt Green was then surrounded by fields and woodland, with hardly any houses nearby. The station was built at the request of the landowning Clive family of nearby Hewell Grange.

Three months earlier, on June 24th, the line had opened between Cheltenham and Bromsgrove, including three minor stations east of Worcester, at Spetchley, Dunhampstead and Droitwich Road. The railway may not have reached Worcester itself, but it was close enough to be of use. A road coach linked the city with Spetchley station. Through tickets for coach and train were issued at the Crown Inn, Broad Street, the coach's city terminus. The coach could carry fifteen passengers and the four mile journey took half an hour. According to a report in the "Worcester Times", the first train on the opening day, with just two carriages, was hauled by a loco named "W.S. Moorsom" (Engineer of the line). Most early locos on the B&G were imported from America, built by William Norris of Philadelphia. This one was a Norris 'Type B', with a 4-2-0 wheel arrangement, a weight of just 8 tons and a price tag of £1,525. The train left Cheltenham at 9.10am and was easily able to travel at 30mph, quite impressive for the time. Stops were made at all stations, including Ashchurch, where a road coach took passengers to and from Tewkesbury. By Defford the train was crammed to capacity. A stop was made at Spetchley, where the locomotive took on water and where road coaches met the train with passengers to and from Worcester.

Four Worcester hotels provided coach connections with the train service - the "Star & Garter" (now the "Star") in Foregate Street, the "Bell Hotel", Angel Place (now demolished), the "Unicorn Inn", Broad Street (later the "Dolphin") and the "Crown",

Broad Street. Passengers could buy a ticket at the hotel valid for the coach and rail journey - a very early example of through ticketing!

By 1845 "Bradshaw's Railway Guide" showed seven trains in each direction. Coaches connected with all of them, even the 1am. departure from Birmingham. A coach left the Crown at 1.41am. with any passengers desperate enough to get to Gloucester at that time of night. The train left Spetchley at 2.17am. and the coach was back at the Crown by 2.47. It is likely that this round trip attracted few passengers, but the 1am. was the southbound mail train, so the coach was important for that purpose alone as it would also carry mails to and from Worcester. In 1845 the northbound mail called at Spetchley at 10.06pm. From the 1830s onwards, the Post Office was quick to appreciate the speed and efficiency of the new railways. The B&G was awarded the contract to carry the mails even before the link into Birmingham was complete. The first mail trains ran on 14th January 1841, a night of driving winds and heavy snow, when the northbound train had to be triple-headed as it made its way slowly up the Lickey Incline. The last Post Office mail train called at Shrub Hill during the 1980s.

The coaches between the Crown and Spetchley ceased after the railway reached Worcester in 1850. Spetchley, Dunhampstead and Droitwich Road all closed to passengers in 1855, although Spetchley saw some excursion trains for visitors to Spetchley Park. The station remained opened for general goods traffic until the end of 1960. Dunhampstead had been served only by the two slow all-stations third class trains in each direction. Before 1852 Droitwich Road was known as 'Droitwich' and it was served by all trains. When the loop through Worcester opened in 1852, together with the real Droitwich station, the fate of Droitwich Road was sealed. However, the station master's house survives to this day, by the bridge carrying the B4090 over the line. To the north, another minor station at Stoke Works closed when the adjacent station on the line from Droitwich opened in 1852. Opening of the line between Droitwich and this new junction at Stoke Works completed the 'Worcester Loop', whereby trains between Bristol and Birmingham could be diverted off the original main line to serve Worcester directly. The southern end of this loop is at Abbotswood Junction, near Norton, and the first section, between the junction and Shrub Hill station, opened in 1850. It was the first part of the Oxford Worcester & Wolverhampton Railway (OWW), which had its headquarters at Shrub Hill.

THE RAILWAY COMES TO WORCESTER

The OWW worked long and hard to justify its nickname of "Old Worse & Worse". It was to be a double track main line, almost ninety miles long, with company headquarters at Worcester. The initial stimulus for building the line seems to have come from some Black Country industrialists, dissatisfied with the service offered by existing railways - the London & Birmingham and the Grand Junction - which they said was unreliable and expensive. They felt it hampered the sale of their goods at home and hindered their export trade through the ports of London and

Peak class diesel electric locomotive No.45149, is seen pausing at Shrub Hill on 16th January 1987, with the last TPO train to stop at Worcester. *(Photo: Stephen Widdowson)*

Castle class No. 7005 "Sir Edward Elgar" is seen next to County class No. 1000 County of Middlesex & Grange Class No.6814 "Enborne Grange" in the Works in May 1962. *(Photo: Ian Catling)*

Liverpool. They saw the new line as an attractive alternative route to London. The Great Western Railway, meanwhile, saw it as a way of breaking into its rivals' territory.

The Great Western's broad gauge main line between Paddington and Bristol had been completed in 1841, and a line off it, from Didcot to Oxford, opened in 1844. To the promoters of the OWW, the Great Western seemed a natural ally and, in September 1844, agreement was reached whereby the GWR would lease the OWW for 999 years. The chief promoters of the line were the Black Country industrialists, plus some Stourbridge glass manufacturers and Kidderminster carpet barons. In September 1844 a prospectus was issued, stating that the OWW would be supported by the experience and resources of the Great Western. It seemed likely to provide handsome profits for those willing to invest in it, but in fact ordinary shareholders were never to receive a penny.

Many public meetings were held as an exercise in selling the idea of the railway. At one such gathering, held in Worcester's Guildhall in 1844, a Stourbridge banker, Francis Rufford, who was to become Chairman of the OWW, extolled the virtues of adopting Brunel's broad gauge for the line. He argued that by this means trains could operate at higher speeds and carry more goods. When the Bill for the OWW was presented to Parliament early in 1845, it enjoyed the enthusiastic support of many people living along its route, together with the backing of the Great Western.

However, this tide of enthusiasm and fund of goodwill must be seen as a high water mark because, even before the Bill was discussed in Parliament, the plot began to unravel. Local enthusiasm for Brunel's 7 foot wide broad gauge, as voiced by Francis Rufford, was not shared by Parliament. By 1844 there were 2175 miles of railway in this country, of which only 274 were broad gauge. For a proper national network to develop, all lines had to be the same gauge. Some MPs were alert to this fact.

The President of the Board of Trade, William Gladstone (later to become Prime Minister four times), announced the Board's disapproval of the OWW, preferring instead plans for a standard gauge route to Worcester, branching off the London & Birmingham line at Tring and passing through Banbury and Evesham. Thus when the Bill for the OWW reached the Committee stage in Parliament, it was examined very carefully indeed. Over one hundred witnesses were called and subjected to a total of 12,148 questions (an average of about 120 each!). Eventually the Committee did report in favour of the broad gauge OWW and the Bill was passed by the Commons by 247 votes to 113. It was given its third and final Commons reading on 24th June 1844. This incensed Richard Cobden, a young radical MP and a strong supporter of a standard national railway gauge. The next day he moved a resolution proposing that a Royal Commission be set up to investigate the gauge question. His proposal was agreed unopposed and the Commission set up on 9th July. It reported in February 1846 and an Act later that year effectively prevented any further spread of the broad gauge, which suffered a long slow decline before final extinction in 1892.

The Act for the OWW received the Royal Assent on 4th August 1845. It stated that the line should be *"formed of such a gauge ... as will admit of the same being worked continuously with the said Great Western Railway"* and be *"constructed and completed in all respects to the satisfaction of the engineer for the time being of the Great Western Railway Company"*.

The Directors of the OWW fancied that their line was destined to become the most important route between the industrial West Midlands and London. This was naive, because it did not serve Birmingham, and in any case the Great Western had other plans. Having reached Oxford from Paddington, it was already behind schemes for lines which would link Oxford with Banbury, Birmingham and Wolverhampton. The Oxford & Rugby (via Banbury), the Birmingham & Oxford Junction, the Birmingham Wolverhampton & Dudley - all had impressive titles but were never meant to be independent. It was always the Great Western's intention to operate these companies' train services and then - after a respectable pause - to absorb them completely. Alerted to this, relations between the Great Western and OWW deteriorated. The Directors of the OWW became reluctant to work with the GWR or indeed to construct its line to the broad gauge.

Shortage of money was another problem, a difficulty that has faced many large construction projects throughout the centuries, from England's medieval cathedrals, including Worcester, down to the Channel Tunnel. The Great Western's engineer, Isambard Kingdom Brunel, had surveyed the route and estimated the total cost of building the railway at £1½million, later revised to £2½ million. The GW Directors agreed that this was the limit of their support for the OWW. However, this was at the height of the 'Railway Mania', with many thousands of men building lines all over the country. The concentrated frenzy of construction, packed into a few brief years in the late 1840s, is unique in the history of transport. Demand for raw materials led to high costs and shortages. The navvies too could demand better wages; if they were refused many migrated to lines where conditions were better. Railway companies that could or would not meet these higher costs saw little activity. In the case of the OWW, the Great Western refused further financial support in 1847, after which the money ran out and work on the line stopped.

The OWW managed to raise an extra £850,000 with the issue of 6% preference shares. On the strength of this Peto & Betts, well established railway contractors, offered to complete the line north of Tipton and south of Worcester within eighteen months. Messrs.Tredwells made a similar offer for the middle section.

Meanwhile, the Birmingham & Gloucester had become part of the Midland Railway. By agreement with the OWW, the Midland built and worked the four mile line from Abbotswood Junction to the joint OWW/Midland station at Worcester Shrub Hill. At first this was a single track standard gauge branch, run as though it were one of the Midland's own. It opened on 5th October 1850. "Berrow's Journal" spoke in the flowery language of the day -

"Tomorrow (Saturday) we people of Worcester shall be able to get into a railway carriage at our own doors and travel to the metropolis without the interposition of any other conveyance, and in consideration of the thing actually being affected, we will endeavour to forget that we have had to wait until the year 1850 before we could do so, and try to forget also all the years of torture we have sustained in the joltings, dust, discomfort and delays of the Spetchley omnibus route. The omnibuses will be engaged in performing services more congenial to their nature - short trips to and from the Tallow Hill station are already more congruous with the idea of a bus than rides of three miles and a half between green hedges. The first passenger train will start from the temporary station on Tallow Hill tomorrow morning at 7.55, and we are glad to say that the arrangements which have been made will obviate the necessity which many people feared would exist, of changing carriages at Abbot's Wood. The carriages from Worcester will not stop there at all but will be taken up to the Spetchley station, there to be attached to the main train..... There will be plenty of conveyances to and from the (Worcester) station, for the rivalry amongst innkeepers is likely to lead to more business in this department than will be profitable. The Mayor has issued a bill requesting omnibus drivers and others in proceeding to the station to go down Sansome Street and to return by way of St.Nicholas Street; an admirable suggestion to prevent confusion. Everything connected with the single line of rails is now in readiness, but the company have only permission to run one engine until the second line shall be completed, which is expected to be in about a week. The station is also in a very forward state, and if not quite finished by tomorrow, will afford sufficient accommodation for the transaction of business and the issue of tickets. It is intended shortly to erect a cattle platform at the station, and a spacious goods shed will also be among the first of the contemplated additions to the temporary erections... "

For the next eighteen months Worcester remained at the end of a branch. There were five trains to and from Bristol and six to Birmingham. The journey to Birmingham, which involved reversal at Abbotswood, attachment to the main train at Spetchley and the ascent of the Lickey Incline, took over two hours. These trains called at Droitwich Road, which continued to be named 'Droitwich' until completion of the loop through the town in 1852. The Midland Railway was keen to complete that loop line and run its expresses through Shrub Hill, but what of the OWW?

Work on the rest of the line was proceeding, but with no sense of urgency and certainly without any wish to co-operate with the Great Western. The OWW was unwilling to lay broad gauge track and in June 1851, after much bitter and inconclusive negotiation, the Great Western offered to work the line, even though they had no standard gauge locos and the OWW had no broad gauge track! OWW shareholders decided to accept this offer if the GWR would buy their £50 shares for £30. As the value of each share had sunk to just £15 the GWR told them exactly where to put them. A few days later, Francis Rufford, former Chairman and still a leading supporter of the OWW, went bankrupt with the failure of his Stourbridge bank and the railway lost £24,000 which it could ill afford.

Thanks to further financial support from the contractor, Peto & Betts, work on the Worcester loop continued in earnest during 1851 and the line opened to traffic on 18th February 1852. Midland Railway expresses now ran through Shrub Hill. The original main line became freight only until 1880, except for two trains each way which called at Droitwich Road, Dunhampstead and Spetchley before they closed to passengers in 1855.

On 1st May 1852 the line opened between Droitwich and Stourbridge and between Worcester and Evesham. The Evesham line deviated from the Abbotswood branch at a new junction at Norton. The formation to Stourbridge was wide enough for broad gauge, even though none was ever laid. This is obvious at some locations today, notably around Hagley. The following year the line between Oxford and Evesham was complete, single track and mixed gauge. The Board of Trade inspector travelled between Oxford and Evesham on 2nd June 1853 and passed the line fit for traffic. It is generally believed that this inspection train was the only one ever to use the broad gauge on the OWW. At the Oxford end of what we now know as the Cotswold Line, there was a branch from Yarnton, south of Hanborough, which joined a London & North Western line at Wolvercot. From 1854 until 1861, this line was the route for a through service between Shrub Hill and London Euston. 1854 also saw completion of the last section of the OWW between Prietfield and Wolverhampton.

It was one thing to open the line; to run a railway properly was quite a different matter! The early history of the OWW is littered with incidents and accidents. Even before the line opened events did not always happen as planned, sometimes because there was no plan. At the beginning of 1852, with construction well advanced and opening through to Stourbridge and Evesham set for May, the OWW owned no locomotives or rolling stock and had no plans for buying any. In March, Brunel resigned as Engineer in sheer exasperation. He was replaced by John Fowler who persuaded C.C.Williams, a London carriage builder, to work the line under contract. Williams contacted the Railway Foundry at Leeds, who sent 27-year old David Joy to Worcester. He was appointed Locomotive Superintendent but on his arrival in April the OWW still had no locos. He scoured the country and by opening day four had arrived, with two more to follow. This assorted rag-bag collection meant that the line opened on time. However, timekeeping nd reliability were very poor. The repair shop at Shrub Hill had virtually no equipment at first.

There were two engine sheds at Shrub Hill, one each for passenger and freight locomotives. In July 1852 the OWW spent £8,500 on 52 acres of land west of the station, on which the locomotive, carriage and wagon works were erected. By

November of that year the first of 20 new locomotives from Hawthorns of Newcastle were delivered, twelve 2-4-0 passenger and eight 0-6-0 freight engines. Unfortunately, a fleet of new locomotives did not necessarily make for an improved railway. Timekeeping and reliability continued to be dire. Brunel's legacy to the OWW was the timber viaducts north of Worcester, notably at Kidderminster and Blakedown (both replaced in the 1880s) and the way the track was supported on longitudinal baulks rather than sleepers. On several occasions, derailed trains were saved from toppling over by the absence of sleepers. In another incident, a loco broke a coupling rod at speed on Hoobrook Viaduct, Kidderminster. The loose rod flailed around, punching holes through the thick deck planking

As on most railways of the time, safety standards were low and signalling was primitive. There were no such things as speedometers and drivers estimated their speed by intelligent guesswork. Joe Leedham, known as "Hell Fire Dick", invariably drove his train as fast as he dared. One night he was approaching the junction at Droitwich from Stourbridge with a heavy coal train. The signal was clear, but it turned to danger right in front of him. In the middle distance, to the left, he saw the southbound mail train approaching from the Stoke Works line. He immediately opened his engine right up and rushed through the junction ahead of the mail, saving both trains. This was in the days before interlocking of points and signals and one can only assume that the signalman must have realised his mistake and quickly set the road for Jack's train again.

On 18th October 1855 the poor timekeeping sank to a new low, even for the OWW. The loco of an Oxford-Wolverhampton express shed a tyre whilst passing through Hartlebury. A second loco arrived within half an hour but its regulator valve promptly developed a fault. The Worcester pilot engine, "Mother Shuter" arrived, but its gauge glass blew out as it attempted to haul the train. A fourth locomotive finally took charge, arriving in Wolverhampton six hours late. Another northbound passenger train had shed a tyre at Hartlebury the previous year. David Joy was informed. He kept a diary of his railway career, which was published in serial form in "Railway Magazine" during 1907-08. It makes lively reading and shows that Joy loved a challenge. On this occasion he was just falling sleep in the 'tied cottage', the company house that came with the job at Shrub Hill. He was woken by the shedman *"tickling my window with the usual long stick with the little bunch of wire at the end"*. Having barked orders to his housekeeper for coffee and toast, he soon organised a breakdown train and set off. *"The traffic department took the passengers and handled them, and we tackled the engine and tender to get them out of the way; it was twelve midnight. As usual, when I had laid my plans, and got all away, I sent a deputation to the nearest 'public' for cans of coffee and bread cut thick, and butter. Men work best on such stuff on cold dark nights; we had big fires and really it was very jolly, but we did not get clear till dawn was showing, around 5am. Then I passed the glasses of beer round and bundled all the men into our breakdown train, to sleep till Worcester. That was alright too."*

The worst accident ever to happen on the OWW was due to sloppy working and sheer negligence. A special train from Wolverhampton to Worcester was promoted as a 'very cheap Sunday school excursion' with a return fare of one shilling (5p) for adults and half that for children. It ran on 23rd April 1858. This double-headed train left Wolverhampton with about 2,000 people on board. Most were in holiday mood, some were crammed into the guard's van and the guard - incredibly - invited them to 'try the brake' in the van. This they did, halting the train three times. Despite this, the train reached Worcester safely. For the return journey, with the rising gradient beyond Stourbridge in mind, it was decided to split the train, running the first part fifteen minutes ahead of the second. As it reached Round Oak, beyond Stourbridge, the guard stepped out of his van just as a coupling broke, causing the rear carriages to roll backwards and brakeless, out of control. The driver of the following train, which was now only ten minutes behind, saw them coming and managed to stop, but the impact was still fearful. Four of the wooden carriages were smashed to splinters, about two hundred people were injured and 14 lost their lives. As the "Birmingham Daily Post" noted, *"The bodies of some of the dead are fearfully mangled and their identification, except by their dress, will in some cases be difficult".*

By the time of the Round Oak tragedy the Old Worse & Worse was coming to the end of its independent existence. Despite its problems it was beginning to expand and thrive. April 1858 was also the month when work began on the Severn Valley Railway, an important branch of the OWW from Hartlebury (not yet Kidderminster) to Bewdley, Bridgnorth and Shrewsbury. In July the following year a single track branch opened from Honeybourne to Stratford-upon-Avon. Plans were drafted for good quality station buildings at Stratford, which resembled a giant Tudor cottage. They were never put into effect there because the OWW branch to Stratford was soon linked across the town with the GW branch from Hatton, and a town centre station provided to a new design. Stratford's OWW branch terminus still existed on paper, of course, and when the basic shack which passed for a station at Kidderminster was destroyed by fire the giant Tudor cottage was built there instead, in 1863, surviving until dry rot forced its demolition a hundred years later.

Another fire destroyed the OWW carriage shed at Shrub Hill after the company had been absorbed by the GWR. The original carriage shed had impressive dimensions - 180 feet long and 42 feet wide. There were sixteen new carriages inside when it caught fire on 11th November 1864. The fire spread rapidly and could not be brought under control, although the appliances at the scene did prevent it from spreading to the workshops, engine sheds and station. The blaze, which could be seen from Malvern, soon attracted thousands of onlookers. According to the special 1pm supplement to the following day's "Berrow's Journal", *"Thousands of men, women and children crowded to Shrub-hill from all quarters of the city, and swarmed on and into empty passenger carriages, loaded goods trains that were stationary and every hill and shed which afforded a vantage ground from which to witness the spectacle. A large number of infants in arms were brought out by their curious mothers..... During the night a county police officer apprehended a man, James Waters, who was carrying off a foot warmer, abstracted from a first class carriage, and the prisoner will be brought before the magistrates."*

After the fire the Great Western abandoned Worcester, Chester and Paddington as carriage building centres, concentrating on Swindon alone.

The whole station area at Shrub Hill always looked very Great Western; to some extent it still does. Despite this, it was a joint station, shared with the Midland Railway. This remained the case right until the formation of British Railways in 1948, although the Midland had become part of the LMS in 1923. During the nineteenth century the Shrub Hill site grew and prospered. It included the station itself, with two full length platforms (253 metres) and four bays. There was an overall roof which lasted until 1935. On the approach from the city the station facade still looks rather like a smaller version of the one at Swindon. It has been spoilt since a hideous concrete office block was dropped in front of it. This monstrosity, which also insults the name of the great Worcester born composer by being named "Elgar House", was built during 1965-66. The site also contained goods sheds - Great Western and Midland - the original OWW engine sheds, goods avoiding lines, locomotive, carriage and wagon works, numerous sidings, stores, etc..

All this was very important but, so far as passengers were concerned, Shrub Hill had one major fault. It was not in the city centre. A convenient central station for Worcester came with the opening of the line to Hereford, although this would never have happened if the original proposals had been carried out.

THE WORCESTER AND HEREFORD LINE

In 1846, at the height of the 'Railway Mania', two rival schemes were proposed for a railway linking Worcester and Hereford. Both sank without trace. In 1852 the London & North Western Railway - eager to tap the South Wales coalfields - presented a Bill before Parliament backing a standard gauge line. This route would have left Worcester by a junction south of Shrub Hill, crossing the Severn and heading directly for Hereford, on a similar alignment to today's A4103 road. Malvern and Ledbury would have been served by single track branch lines, that to Malvern having gradients as steep as 1:30.

The Bill failed, but the LNWR came back the next year with a new scheme, devised by Charles Liddell, Engineer of the Newport Abergavenny & Hereford Railway (NA&H). Liddell had presented the earlier scheme, but by now he realised that merely to join Worcester and Hereford was not sufficient. To be viable it had to directly serve Malvern and Ledbury, the only places of consequence between the two cities. A line to Malvern could best leave Worcester north of Shrub Hill, thereby providing the means for a station in the city centre.

This was the best route for a line between Worcester and Hereford, but it was also the most expensive. The brick viaduct between Shrub Hill and the Severn would involve considerable demolition of property. There were to be two lengthy tunnels, at Colwall and Ledbury, and another brick viaduct at Ledbury. The line had the support of the Corporations of Worcester and Hereford, and the citizens of Malvern and Ledbury. The Bill passed through the House of Commons intact. The Lords, in their wisdom, thought differently, insisting that the Worcester & Hereford should be a genuinely independent railway and deleting all clauses which permitted financial support from the LNWR or any other railway. The Bill became an Act, but without the ability to call on outside backing, very little work was done on this 'independent' line, although construction of Colwall Tunnel was begun. During 1858 the Directors of the Worcester & Hereford, OWW and NA&H met and decided to work together to raise funds for the construction of the line. (These three companies amalgamated on 1st July 1860 to form the West Midland Railway, which was absorbed by the Great Western in 1863.) This funding, together with additional support from the Midland Railway - keen, like the LNWR, to gain access to South Wales - meant that work could begin in earnest after the funding was given legal authority by an Act of 2nd August 1858.

The most difficult undertaking on the route was the construction of Colwall Tunnel, 1,567 yards long on a 1:80 gradient through the Malvern Hills. The contractor was Stephen Ballard, of Colwall. The core of the hills consists of an extremely hard and ancient rock, syenite. At first, progress on the tunnel was measured at about ten metres a week, but when contact was made with the syenite, the bore moved forward at less than a metre a week. Ballard twice sub-contracted some of the tougher excavating, but both sub-contractors soon gave up. A steam-driven tunnelling device was tried. It had been used, without success, to undermine the walls of Sebastopol in the Crimean War and it fared no better at Colwall. The tunnellers intercepted springs, causing danger to themselves and the loss of well water to people living above. Eventually, on 21st July 1860, the two faces met and Stephen Ballard, along with some of the Directors, was able to walk through.

The tunnel had been difficult to construct and it caused problems later. A rock fall closed it for a week in November 1907. The brick lining continued to decay, helped by the blast from locomotive chimneys. After the First World War the Great Western decided to construct a new tunnel parallel to the old. Work began in 1924 and the new tunnel opened on 2nd August 1926. It has a larger bore and is on an easier gradient, 1:90 instead of 1:80. The new tunnel is 22 yards longer than the old, and close enough to use the original ventilation shafts by means of cross bores. The old tunnel found a new lease of life during the Second World War, when it served as a 'Naval Armaments Store', where all sorts of bombs, warheads and explosives were stored, generally for one or two days, before onward distribution. A consignment of '43 loose bombs', for example, was received from Woolwich on 16th March 1940, before dispatch on 18th. During 1941 a narrow gauge (1' 6") line was laid within the tunnel to ease storage and movement of the ammunition. It was worked by two Ruston & Hornsby diesel locomotives, which had a top speed of 9½mph.

The tunnel at Ledbury, at 1,323 yards, is shorter than Colwall Tunnel, although it too is on a rising gradient towards the line summit at Colwall station. The bore is narrow and unlined. A little to the west is Ledbury Viaduct, 330 yards long and 60 feet high. Its 31 arches consumed over five million bricks, all made on site. On 12th June 1861 the last brick was keyed into place. A single track from the west was complete, enabling guests from Hereford to arrive by train for the ceremony. The line was opened throughout on 17th September that year, with completion of the lining of Colwall Tunnel. Stephen Ballard and his guests rode through the tunnel for a banquet at his home, 'The Winnings', which is above the west portal. There were four trains a day at first, generally taking 100 minutes for the 29 miles. As "Berrows Journal" noted, *"Simultaneously with the opening of the Worcester & Hereford Railway the mail coach between those towns ceased on Friday its daily journeys, succumbing at once to the invincible competition, steam"*.

At the Worcester end, the first section of line had opened in the summer of 1859. A new 2-2-2 locomotive had arrived, fresh from Stephenson's works at Newcastle, together with some rolling stock. A single track was ready between Henwick and Malvern Link, but the line between Shrub Hill and Henwick was not. So that a train service could start, the engine and stock were hauled from Shrub Hill through the city streets, over the road bridge and on to Henwick, where they were re-railed. Photography was still in its infancy, so there is no known record of what must have been a spectacular street procession. The train service began, with horse bus connections between Shrub Hill and Henwick, and between Malvern Link, Great Malvern and Malvern Wells.

The two arch bridge across the Severn was inspected by Colonel Yolland of the Board of Trade late in 1859. He refused to pass it as fit for traffic, as he was concerned about the deflection of the arches when a train passed over it. Strengthening work was carried out and, after a further inspection, the bridge was opened on 17th May 1860, together with Foregate Street station. Shrub Hill has always been the focal point of railway activities in Worcester, but Foregate Street is in the centre of the city. The two platforms are on a curve and the architecture is pure Great Western. Between 1889 and 1959 a signalbox straddled the platforms and a footbridge provided an alternative to the subway. Two attractive features of today's station are the small platform-end cafe near the bridge over Foregate Street, and the bridge itself. Seen from the street, this bridge was once of the plain girder type, but the present more elaborate frame, with coloured crests of the GWR and the city, was installed in 1909. The city council had voted £162 towards this improvement. A photograph, taken on Sunday 2nd May, shows the work in hand. The bridge carries a large warning - "Caution, keep your seats while passing under this bridge" - for the benefit of top deck tramcar passengers. The main bridge over the Severn, like Colwall Tunnel, did not wear well. It was replaced by the present girder viaduct in 1905, which makes use of the original abutments and pier.

Although never a joint station, Foregate Street did see Midland Railway trains, if only in passing. The Midland ran four trains per day between Shrub Hill and Hereford from 1869. As they called only at Malvern Link, Great Malvern and Ledbury, they were of no use to Foregate Street passengers.

The line to Hereford also provided Worcester with a very useful suburban station, at Henwick. There was a busy goods yard here and the station, with attractive gardens, was fully staffed. The suburban service on this side of the city grew in the early part of the twentieth century. Main line trains were supplemented by locals to Malvern Wells and along the Bromyard line. By 1932 the original stations between Worcester and Malvern Link - at Henwick and Bransford Road - had been supplemented by halts at Boughton, Rushwick and Newland. Local trains towards Malvern, all of which served Henwick, left Foregate Street at the following times -

07.20 07.40 07.50 08.10(B) 08.20 08.37 08.43(H) 09.45 10.24 10.32(B) 11.19 12.30 13.00 13.20(B) 13.45 14.25(B) 14.34 15.14 16.14 16.30 17.32(B) 17.40 18.23 19.37(B) 19.50 20.25 22.15 23.00(H - Th&SO) 23.10(Th&SO)

(B) = train for the Bromyard line : (H) = train terminates at Henwick :

(Th&SO) = Thursdays and Saturdays only

The station at Henwick really came into its own during the severe flooding of 1947, when the Severn rose to seventeen feet above normal. For four days, 19th-22nd March, there were only two ways to travel from one side of the city to the other. Some people clambered aboard lorries which ploughed past the county cricket ground through four feet of water. Many more used the train. The GWR ran an emergency shuttle service between Henwick and Foregate Street every fifteen minutes, using a diesel railcar. All other trains called at both these stations. Local trains normally had only three carriages, but some were strengthened to eight. In this way thousands of extra passengers were carried across the river - all in complete safety although not necessarily on time. The railway ran out of tickets, so the Midland Red supplied bus tickets, which were used until more rail tickets could be printed.

The station closed in 1965 and was demolished in 1967. The signal box at the level crossing, dating from 1875, remains busy. From time to time there have been plans, discussions and debates about providing a new station at Henwick. There has been at least one scheme for a park and ride station and various consultations about who should pay for what. It is time to cut through the wasted years of red tape. A station here - park and ride or otherwise - would be well used by the many people who live within walking distance and who are tired of the congested journey into the city by road. The road bridge over the Severn is a single point for all traffic from Henwick. A new station would provide a welcome relief for the local community on this side of the river, although it wouldn't be necessary, this time, to provide two late trains ten minutes apart on Thursday and Saturday nights!

BRANCHES & WORKS

There were two unusual freight branches within the city of Worcester. One was the Lowesmoor Tramway, always known as the Vinegar Branch. It opened in 1872 and was about 900 yards long, running from within the triangle of lines north of Shrub Hill, down to Hill Evans' Vinegar Works near the city centre. Despite its official name, its route did not take it to the road known as Lowesmoor. It crossed the main line between Shrub Hill and Foregate Street on a flat crossing, bridged Tolladine Road and passed to the side of Heenan & Froude's engineering works, formerly McKenzie & Holland. A spur from the branch gave access to Heenan & Froude, passing very close to the side of Holy Trinity church as it did so. The Vinegar Branch then crossed Shrub Hill Road on the level, continued over the canal and level crossing at Padmore Street and Pheasant Street before arriving at the works. The continuous incline down from Shrub Hill meant that special attention had to be given to ensure safe operation. The branch had several unique features. The maximum load was twelve vans, plus a guard's van at both ends. Shrub Hill Road crossing was protected on both sides by catch points. These were released when a shunter who walked down from the station had alerted road traffic by setting the road signals to danger. These were not conventional traffic lights, but standard Great Western lower quadrant railway signals - they did not feature in any copy of the Highway Code. Train speed crossing the road was 4mph. Before Padmore Crossing, adjacent to the Midland Red bus depot, the train stopped and the brakes were applied on the leading guard's van. The loco, a GW pannier tank, uncoupled and ran forward onto a spur. The gates over Padmore Street were normally closed by a designated vinegar works employee, who knew there was a train on the branch when the Shrub Hill Junction signalman activated a gong which sounded in the factory. After satisfying himself that the gates were indeed closed to road traffic, the guard on the leading van released the brake and the engine less train continued by gravity alone, often crossing Pheasant Street at 20mph and with very little sound. An adapted tractor, fitted with rail wheels and buffers, shunted within the works, while the pannier tank followed later to collect the train. On one occasion, according to an account in "Old Worcester as seen through the camera" (Hayes, pub.Barracuda), a steam roller collided with the tank engine on Pheasant Street crossing - the steam roller lost. Both guard's vans were marshalled at the rear for the return journey, as extra insurance against a runaway on the incline. The round trip was booked to take 45 minutes. There was one daily working, Mondays to Fridays, the last train running on Friday 5th June 1964.

Between Foregate Street station and the Severn, a substantial single track viaduct, 553 yards long, broke away from the main line, descending to the river on a steep incline and sharp curve. This was the Butts Branch, which continued north along the river bank to Butts Terminus, alongside the Grandstand Hotel at the racecourse. There were cattle pens at the terminus and the branch also played a vital role in transporting horses on race days. Its other important function should have been to provide a means of exchanging freight between the railway and river craft. For this purpose an arm of the branch went south under the viaduct and along the riverside, past the present car park and moorings for pleasure boats, under an arch of the river bridge, to the south quay. When the branch was built there were plans to extend it further, past the cathedral, but opposition from the cathedral authorities ensured that this part was never built. When the road bridge was rebuilt in 1932, the riverside line was cut back to a point near what is now Newport Street bus station. This section fell into disuse soon afterwards and, on the main part of the branch, facilities for racehorse owners were withdrawn in April 1953. A small section of the viaduct remains, near where it left the main line at what was Butts Branch Junction.

The firm of Heenan & Froude was based in the factory that had been founded as the Vulcan Iron Works in 1857. The Vulcan Works, in Cromwell Street, was owned by McKenzie & Holland and it was an important railway signalling works. By the beginning of the twentieth century it covered over five acres and provided work for more than six hundred men, making it one of the largest employers in the city. The works' first signal designer was F.W.Comber, who had invented an early 'lock and block' system, 'locking' signals and points with each other so that, for instance, junction signals and points could not be moved independently of and contrary to each other. The system of interlocking was developed and refined throughout the rest of the nineteenth century. By 1900 most British railway companies were using McKenzie & Holland equipment to some extent. It also played a large part in the safe running of railways in many parts of the British Empire, especially India, South Africa, Australia and New Zealand, as well as other countries where the railways were largely British built, such as Egypt and Argentina.

"Berrows Journal" issued an 'industrial supplement' in 1903, informing readers of all the city's industries, great and small. Of McKenzie & Holland it says -

"They are the patentees and contractors for the manufacture and erection of railway signals, patent interlocking apparatus and signal work of every description. They also make and erect signalmen's cabins in brick, stone or wood; signal posts in wood, iron or steel ..... combined electric telegraph block and interlocking apparatus; cast iron water tanks, water cranes and columns .... They are also sole licensees for the manufacture in Great Britain of Sykes' combined electric block locking and the principal agents in this Kingdom and the Colonies for the Westinghouse electro-pneumatic system of signalling and inter-locking apparatus, a separate department for the manufacture of the latter having recently been added..... To insure the uniform thoroughness and excellent condition of their appliances, Messrs.McKenzie & Holland make all the various parts themselves, nothing being let out on contract or otherwise to other firms...... It is not too much to say that they have materially assisted in the development of the most distant countries, by providing apparatus which facilitates the construction and the safe

Bulldog class loco No.3353, "Pershore Plum". (Photo: Jack Saunders collection)

GWR railcar No.20 is seen at Henwick in the Summer of 1957. (Photo: David Badham)

economical management of railways."

McKenzie & Holland may have gone, along with a flowery and fussy way of writing, but their equipment has stood the test of time on some lines where power boxes have not replaced mechanical signalling. As well as the more remote parts of India and Argentina, for example, McKenzie & Holland signalling frames are still busy locally, in the boxes at Henwick, Hartlebury and Ledbury.

The whole area around Shrub Hill was the focus of railway life in the city. Here were the original two OWW engine sheds, loco, carriage and wagon repair shops, extensive marshalling yards and both Great Western and Midland goods sheds. There were six mechanical signal boxes, all open round the clock. The locomotive repair shops, built in the nineteenth century, had not expanded sufficiently to meet the needs of the twentieth; larger locos undergoing repair had to leave their tenders outside. The sheds (shed code 'WOS' in Great Western days; 85A under British Railways) were brick built. The passenger engine shed had three through running lines and was unusual in that it was on a curve, although the tracks were straight within the shed. The goods loco shed had four terminal roads; it was situated alongside the Foregate Street-Tunnel Junction side of the 'Worcester Triangle'. By the last year of the Great Western's independent existence - 1947 - Worcester had a mixed complement of pannier tanks of assorted vintage, plus freight, mixed traffic and express locos, the latter featuring members of the 'Star', 'Castle', 'Hall' and 'Grange' classes. The shed closed to steam in December 1965, following a slow decline after the Second World War. In 1947 there were 91 locos shedded here, although one of Worcester's more celebrated engines had been withdrawn the previous year. This was a member of the 4-4-0 'Bulldog' Class, No.3353, built in 1900. Originally named "Plymouth", it was renamed "Pershore Plum" in 1927 on the centenary of the discovery of this wild type of yellow plum. 3353 was shedded at Worcester for its entire career. The number of locos allocated to 85A had dropped to 82 by 1950, 79 by 1959 and just 24 by April 1964.

The amount of general freight was considerable. In 1938 the yard handled 185,000 tons of freight, of which 5,000 tons was vinegar, with 2,000 tons of Worcester Sauce from Lea & Perrins, 10,000 tons of tins and tinplate and 8,000 tons of machinery. In addition, Shrub Hill handled three-quarters of a million parcels that year. Even as late as 1960, 950 wagons were handled at Worcester during an average day, although a survey highlighted a key weakness of wagonload traffic and large marshalling yards - no less than 58% of these wagons were handled by two or more locomotives. (Stories of wagons being 'lost' and shunted around marshalling yards for days or even weeks were not entirely without foundation.) The 1960s brought the cold reality of the Beeching era, ruthless closures and a struggle towards a more efficient railway. Worcester felt the full effect.

TRAIN SERVICES

The Great Western Railway was known to its many admirers as 'God's Wonderful

Railway', but for the first part of the twentieth century there were few improvements to the speed of its main line service between Worcester and London. The 1932 summer time-table, for example, shows the first up train leaving Shrub Hill at 06.35 and arriving at Paddington at 09.50. The 08.55 was, along with the 14.00, the fastest train of the day, taking 2 hours 20 minutes for the 120 miles to Paddington. The 08.55 began at Hereford at 7.25, with a portion leaving Kidderminster at 08.09, the forerunner of the 'Cathedrals Express'. On the LMS line to Birmingham, most important trains by-passed Worcester. Local trains on this difficult route up the Lickey Incline took over an hour to cover the 24 miles. The first train to Birmingham, the 08.14 from Shrub Hill, arrived in New Street at 09.25, the following 09.05 departure omitted some stations, reaching Birmingham at 10.00.

The Great Western's major innovation of the 1930s was the streamlined diesel railcar. A prototype began running on the local service between Reading and Paddington in 1933. The following year three cars, each with two AEC engines of the type then fitted to London Transport buses, began an express service between Birmingham Snow Hill and Cardiff via the Honeybourne line, calling only at Gloucester Central and Newport. With smart acceleration and a top speed of 80mph these trains were 35 minutes faster than the best steam express on the same route. They were an instant hit with passengers, despite a fare supplement of half a crown (12½p). Further diesel railcars were built, totalling 38 by the time production ceased in 1943. Car No.19 was the first to have modified streamlining, being angular rather than rounded. Two of the later cars were for parcels only and some were twin units, foreshadowing the diesel multiple units of the 1950s. The three cars built for the Cardiff service each had a buffet, but later cars did not. They had thirty more seats instead and, from 1935, some were put to work between Oxford, Worcester and Hereford. Soon they were also providing services from Worcester to Stratford and Leamington via Honeybourne, on the Bromyard line and along the Severn Valley Line via Hartlebury. Worcester normally had an allocation of seven railcars, more than any other shed.

Two days before the outbreak of the Second World War the first batch of evacuees arrived at Shrub Hill from Birmingham. The following day further trains arrived with over two hundred mothers and their babies from three of Birmingham's maternity hospitals. The threat of invasion in 1940 saw the formation of the Local Defence Volunteers, soon renamed the Home Guard. Worcester railway workers, like other able bodied men not actually in the forces, were members of the Home Guard. The top of the water tower in the goods yard was the best vantage point from which to spot German aircraft, although thankfully Worcester suffered virtually no enemy action during the war. No bombs fell on the railway although an ammunition train was 'chased' by a bomber apparently returning from a raid on Birmingham. Fortunately, the train was entering Rainbow Hill Tunnel at the time!

During the war inter-company rivalries were forgotten as locomotives, of whatever company, were sent wherever they could be of most use. Few railway photographs

A wartime photo taken in the 1940's of a USA class S160 No. 1621,stabled opposite Worcester coaling stage. The large water tower in the top right of the picture was taken down in March 2000.

(Photo : Courtesy of J.A Peden)

3MT 0-6-0, No. 2249 stands in Platform 1, the north bay at Shrub Hill,& a Swindon built class 120 DMU can be seen on platform 2 in this photo taken in 1962. The north bay has since been filled in, & is now the staff carpark.

(Photo: Bob Sim)

At the start of the 2nd World War, Shrub Hill's Home Guard are seen in front of the station. Out of the 66 faces in this photo, the following 34 names are known:- F.Bright,G. Truby, J. Pardoe,C Fields,C Milner, P. Stanton,R. Church,L. Williams,G. Heath,S. Ayres,A. Marshall, A. Parker,L. Watkins,W. Rodway, J. Brace,A. Penfold,H. Crutch F. Inight,F. Hill,R. Arch, W. Vickers,W. Smith,R. Pardoe,F. Barnett,W. Hunt,E. Newman,Wintle,M. Harding, D. Burston,T. Hine,Freeman,P. Wall,Finch & Norman Holiday.

(Photo: Courtesy of John Pardoe)

Token's for the single line section between Norton Jct & Evesham, can be given up by, or handed to the driver at both Norton signal box or Worcester Shrub Hill station, where the machine is in a small hut on the platform. This is so that trains can be given "right of way" at Worcester SH for Evesham, & do not have to stop at Norton. To obtain a token at Shrub Hill the station chargeman has to get permission from Norton Box, who presses a button to release a token at Shrub Hill. Station chargeman Trevor Lettice is seen obtaining a token on 29/3/98. (Photo: Stephen Widdowson)

A photo showing the Joint Station uniform with the WJS standing for (Worcester Joint Station) Albert Roan is standing, (he was known as Tim) (Photo: Courtesy of Mrs Ruth Poole)

were taken and they were not encouraged. Nevertheless, a handful have survived, including a colour shot of Worcester shed in 1943, showing locos from the Great Western, LMS, LNER and Southern Railway. New 'Austerity' War Department (WD) heavy freight 2-8-0 locomotives were introduced in 1942, based on Stanier's 'Black Five' design for the LMS. Over nine hundred were eventually built. They were used on all parts of the system, including lines through Worcester. Much rarer were American wartime visitors, Class S160 2-8-0 heavy freight engines built by Alco, Baldwin and Lima for the US Army and imported for use in Britain from December 1942. Some 174 were loaned to the Great Western and a few passed through Worcester during the course of their duties. All were handed back to the US Army late in 1944 for use in Europe as the allies advanced.

Wartime passenger services were severely pruned. The 1944-45 winter time-table, for instance, showed few trains from Worcester to Birmingham New Street, with huge gaps between them. The 08.23 from Shrub Hill was followed by the 13.06, after which the next train left at 17.48.

The railways slowly recovered from the effects of the war years. On 1st January 1948 the GWR became part of the new nationalised network, British Railways (the 'ways' was not dropped until the 1960s). Shrub Hill was no longer a joint station, but firmly within the Western Region of BR. The influence of the ghost of the Great Western could be seen when new chocolate and cream name signs were introduced at all three Worcester stations during the 1950s. After nationalisation, a new carmine and cream livery, known as 'blood and custard', was adopted for main line carriages throughout the country but by the end of the 1950s the regions were going their own nostalgic way, with the Southern resurrecting malachite green and the Western following suite with chocolate and cream.

Green of another shade - given the exciting name 'rail green' - was the livery for the new diesel railcars which were built in huge numbers as part of the Modernisation Plan of 1955. They were first seen at Worcester in 1956, with the dieselisation of the Snow Hill-Cardiff service, routed via Kidderminster, Worcester and Hereford. It was operated by Class 120 Swindon built 'Cross Country' dmus, which had corridor connections, toilets and buffets. They ran semi-fast between Birmingham and Worcester, calling only at Smethwick West, Stourbridge Junction, Kidderminster and Droitwich. No Class 120 dmu has been preserved. Dmus built specifically for Western Region local services began appearing at Worcester in 1957, mixing with steam and Great Western railcars at first. Initially they had no corridors, but these were provided in later years, thanks to the twin problems of vandalism and the need for the guard to issue tickets to passengers boarding at unstaffed stations. Some of these units survived in the Brmingham area until 1994.

At first the new trains attracted new passengers, but the effect was only temporary. More people were earning more money, in real terms, than ever before. When Prime Minister Harold Macmillan was famously quoted in 1957, as saying 'You've never had it so good' he was right. More people could afford to buy the ultimate symbol of progress and independence - a car. Similarly, the railway's freight customers were less and less willing to tolerate the delays and inefficiency that were endemic in the goods yards of the time. The M1 had opened in 1959, the first part of the M5, with the M50, opened in 1962 and road hauliers could offer a keen competitive service. The railways of Worcester, like railways everywhere, were soon feeling the draught of harsh reality.

The first part of the goods yard closed at the end of 1960, followed by the Vinegar branch and the locomotive repair shops in 1964, and the short but important branch to the gas works and Underwoods coal yard in 1965. The railway sheeting works at Shrub Hill were gutted by fire on 16th October 1967 and the railway workshops, having closed, were demolished during April 1969. The shed closed to steam in 1965 and the following summer, during the rush to abandon steam, a locomotive was actually scrapped in the city. 0-6-0 3F tank engine No.47681 developed a hot box while being hauled to Cashmore's scrapyard at Newport. It was detached from the train of dead locomotives and briefly stored at Worcester before being cut up on site. 47681 was an ex-LMS 'Jinty', the last numbered of a class of over 400. They were designed by Henry Fowler in 1924 and a few could always be seen at Bromsgrove, clustered at the foot of the Lickey Incline as they waited to do banking duty.

The first major passenger closure occurred in July 1962, when services ceased between Stourbridge Junction and Priestfield (junction with the Birmingham-Wolverhampton line). Although some distance from Worcester, this was the northern end of the original OWW main line and there were through trains between Worcester and Wolverhampton right up until closure. Most consisted of just three or four carriages, but they could sometimes be seen hauled by an immaculate member of the "Castle" Class, running in after overhaul at Wolverhampton and before return to more normal duties.

The last steam-hauled local train to Worcester from Birmingham Snow Hill ran on Friday 4th September 1964, hauled by a "County" class engine, still a youngster at less than twenty years old. During the 1950s the Western Region had named many of its more important trains. In 1957, the early morning Hereford-Paddington train became the "Cathedrals Express", complete with locomotive headboard. Normal formation was five coaches from Hereford, with three coaches from Kidderminster attached at Shrub Hill, plus a restaurant car. This procedure operated in reverse in the evening. The last "Cathedrals Express" ran in 1965. The Hereford-Worcester-Paddington expresses were now dieselised, briefly in the hands of the ill-fated diesel-hydraulic "Hymek" and "Warship" classes, the Hymeks lasting until September 1973. From 1973 most Worcester-Paddington trains were hauled by Class 31s, which proved to be underpowered. The busiest train of the week, the Sunday evening Hereford-Paddington did not have extra coaches added at Shrub Hill; the whole train ran from Hereford and was double-headed throughout. Most

A rare photograph of Boughton Halt, the next station after Henwick .　　　(Photo: Ian Catling)

Diesel Hydraulic (Hymek) locomotive No. D7077 is seen at Shrub Hill on 22nd March 1972, with the 14.15 service to Paddington. (Note the BRUTES on the platform.)　　(Photo: Brian Harris)

31s were soon found work elsewhere and many trains on the route were worked by that successful maid-of-all-work, the Class 47 and then followed by Class 50's, until the High Speed Trains (HSTs) came to the line. The "Cathedrals Express" name was revived for the most important Hereford-Worcester-Paddington train of the day on 13th May 1985, although the HSTs which operate the service do not carry a headboard.

The cross country branch to Bromyard and Leominster had opened in 1897 and trains normally started from the 'Leominster bay' at the north end of Shrub Hill. Trains travelled towards Malvern on the main line until the branch peeled off at Leominster Junction, just north of Bransford Road station. The service was cut back to Bromyard in 1952. Its survival for twelve more years was due in part to the lack of parallel bus services. Normal services ceased on Saturday 5th September 1964 but the line closed in flamboyant style the following day. Bill Morris, of Morris Coaches of Bromyard, organised a special train from Bromyard to Blackpool for a fare of just one guinea (£1.05). Demand was so great that over 80 people had to be turned away. On the train, there was accordion music and bingo sessions to entertain the passengers, who finally arrived back at Bromyard at 1.35am the following morning.

Some stations and halts in the Worcester area had closed before the 1960s. Surely the shortest lived was Astwood Halt, north of Worcester, which opened in 1936 and shut as a wartime economy measure in 1939. The vast majority of station closures occurred in the 1960s, reaching a peak in 1965. Closures that year included most remaining halts on the routes radiating from Shrub Hill. These were Boughton Halt, Rushwick Halt, Bransford Road and Newland Halt on the Malvern line, and Fernhill Heath, Cutnall Green and Stoke Works north of the city. The staffed stations at Malvern Wells and Henwick also closed that year. Norton Junction closed at the beginning of 1966 and Honeybourne followed when the Worcester to Stratford-upon-Avon local service was withdrawn in May 1969. Honeybourne subsequently re-opened as a halt, served by some Worcester-Oxford trains, in May 1981. Some stations which survived had their services reduced to almost nothing; Bromsgrove and Pershore were both provided with one train a day in each direction. Worcester Foregate Street was closed on Sundays from 1965, very inconvenient for people needing to visit the city centre or make bus connections. The Sunday train service was restored in 1985, although the travel centre had been staffed on Sundays for over a year previously. Frustrated would-be passengers could buy their tickets at Foregate Street and hear the trains trundle overhead without stopping, before making their way on foot to Shrub Hill.

The 1970s saw further economies and cutbacks. Train services suffered but so too did the track layout. Within Worcester, the track and signalling were 'rationalised' (ie; 'downgraded') between Shrub Hill and Henwick during 1973. The former double track through Foregate Street station became two single tracks; one between Henwick and Shrub Hill and the other forming a Shrub Hill avoiding line for trains travelling between the Malvern line and Birmingham. The old triangle of lines at Worcester is no more. Trains between Hereford and Birmingham can call at either of Foregate Street's platforms and in either direction, depending on whether they also serve Shrub Hill. This can be very confusing for people unfamiliar with the station. The track layout also hampers efficient running at busy times and delays can quickly develop if a train is late or runs out of sequence. The track layout, although dating only from 1973, is still controlled by lower quadrant semaphore signalling.

The Worcester-Hereford line once had just two sections of single track, through Colwall and Ledbury tunnels. The stretch between the tunnels was singled in October 1967; the longer section from Ledbury to Shelwick Junction, on the approach to Hereford, was singled in 1984.

The most serious case of track singling, now more than ever seen as a false economy, took place on the Cotswold Line in 1971. Over fifty miles of this main line, between Norton Junction and Wolvercote Junction (just north of Oxford) was singled, except for the eleven miles between Moreton-in-Marsh and Ascott-under-Wychwood and a passing loop at Evesham. The potential for delay is considerable and, before the arrival of the HSTs and the Turbo DMUs, the older trains often wrestled unsuccessfully with the time-table and the track layout. It is 86 miles by rail between Hereford and Oxford; almost 60 of them are now single track. Soon after singling of the Cotswold Line, British Rail made further attempts to downgrade the line. Regular freight traffic ceased with singling and it was decided to place all passenger services in the charge of diesel multiple units, as these would cause less wear on the track than locomotives. They would shuttle between Hereford, Worcester and Oxford only, with effect from May 1982. These were, of course, the tired old 1950s DMUs, not the Turbo units familiar on the line today. British Rail, its hands tied behind its back by H.M.Treasury, seemed unable to grasp that the drop in passenger numbers that this would have undoubtedly brought about would have more than cancelled out any savings made by less wear on the track. The line's very active user group, the Cotswold Line Promotion Group, formed in 1978, fought a long, hard, and ultimately successful campaign to ensure that the four most important trains of the day would still be locomotive hauled and that they would run through between Hereford, Worcester and Paddington. Terminal decline was narrowly avoided.

The service linking Worcester with Birmingham, on both lines, also suffered serious decline. After 1971 there were no trains outside the peak hours between Worcester and Kidderminster. The local service on the Bromsgrove route was virtually non-existent and the few Bristol-Birmingham trains which ran via Shrub Hill reverted to the main line during the 1970s.

Gradually the fortunes of the railways in the Worcester area improved. Re-opening at Honeybourne in May 1981, and the slow but relentless improvement to the service at Pershore were straws in the wind. In 1983 the service to Birmingham was recast, with an hourly train via Kidderminster running semi-fast. The success of these trains - with a 300% increase in Worcester-Kidderminster ticket sales within six months - soon led to further improvements that would have seemed crazy even five years earlier. The Birmingham semi-fast trains ran half hourly, some running through to Great Malvern and Hereford. In 1987, one of the semi-fasts was extended past Worcester Shrub Hill every two hours, not to Malvern, but to Gloucester, Chepstow and Cardiff, providing a regular service on another of Worcester's neglected passenger routes. After a successful year these trains were diverted via the Bromsgrove line, but without reducing the frequency of trains via Kidderminster.

The improvements of the 1980s, consolidated during the 1990s, were only possible because of the introduction of a whole series of new diesel multiple unit trains. Although the enhanced Kidderminster line service began with vintage stock in 1983, the introduction of Class 150 Sprinters from 1985 meant greater reliability. Only then was the frequency doubled. These trains, now in their green Centro livery, remain a familiar sight on the Kidderminster line. The Cardiff service was operated by Class 155 'Super Sprinters', but most of these two car units were soon modified to run as single cars. Reclassified as Class 153, most work outside the area, although they can occasionally be seen at Worcester. A Class 153 unit always works the Stourbridge shuttle, the so-called 'Town Car' as the platform at Stourbridge Town is too short for anything else. Later Sprinters include the Class 156 and 158, both of which work through Worcester, chiefly on the Birmingham-Cardiff service. Before the end of the twentieth century, frequency on the Cardiff route had become hourly with some trains extended through Birmingham to Nottingham. Many stations which local users would like to see re-opened - such as Henwick, Malvern Wells, Campden - remain closed. A useful exception is on the Bristol/Cardiff line, where the long gap between Worcester and Cheltenham was plugged with the opening of the £1.2 million station at Ashchurch in May 1997. The Cardiff service is seeing further improvements with the introduction of more new stock, the Class 170 dmus in the distinctive new Central Trains livery. These are being phased in during 2000.

The Cotswold Line Promotion Group's campaign to retain loco hauled trains to Paddington was won in 1982, yet they only lasted for two more years. However, this was not a betrayal, but an improvement, as High Speed Trains were introduced in 1984. Other Cotswold Line services are now provided by new Class 166 Turbo DMUs. Their superior speed and acceleration brought about a tightening of the time-table and more through running to and from Paddington. They enabled some stations to be better served within the constraints of the long sections of single track. Nowhere is this more obvious than at Hanborough, the last halt before Oxford. During the late 1960s and 70s, this halt 'enjoyed' the same service as others along the line, normally two trains per day up to Oxford, with one evening return. Now all Turbo services call there. Success has brought its own problems, as the car park is frequently overfull.

On the route to Birmingham it has been possible, since 1995, to travel from Worcester to Birmingham Snow Hill via a re-opened stretch of railway, known as the 'Jewellery Line', complete with three new stations. Along the Hereford line, there are two trains to Birmingham every hour from Great Malvern for much of the day, with an approximately hourly service from Hereford itself. Not all improvements were successful, although failures have been few. A New Street-Stourbridge-Worcester-Paddington Turbo service was started in October 1993, one train a day in each direction. It ran off-peak and was not well marketed; the down train was withdrawn in 1994, the up service lasting until May 1995. And who now remembers a brave but short-lived experiment tried some years earlier, when an evening commuter train from Birmingham split at Shrub Hill, two cars providing a through service to Pershore and Evesham?

The improvements to the train services are now, at the time of writing, being followed by enhancements to the railway itself. All stations, to a greater or lesser extent, are being improved, nowhere more so than Shrub Hill itself.

There are many things remaining to be done. The city would benefit from two new stations, at Henwick and to the east of the city, a parkway station where the Cotswold Line crosses the B&G main line near Norton Junction. The signalling, a legacy of the nineteenth century, needs to be brought into the twenty-first. The track layout is a legacy of the cutbacks of the 1960s and 70s. Restoration of conventional double track through Foregate Street would improve reliability of the service. The Cotswold Line time-table between Worcester and Paddington is more frequent than ever, with no fewer than 13 trains to London every weekday, 4 starting back from Hereford and 8 from Great Malvern. It is difficult to see how further improvements can be sustained without re-doubling some of the track between Worcester and Oxford. These are problems, but at least they are the problems of growth; Worcester's railways are no longer in decline.

TALES OF SHRUB HILL

Edward 'Ted' Clissold's earliest memories of Worcester Shrub Hill go right back to 1910. He was eight years old and would sometimes travel to Worcester with his mother, from Norton Junction. Two pictures of Shrub Hill station stand out in his mind from those distant days. In the absence of a public footbridge, passengers literally crossed the tracks. The platforms dipped to rail level and the crossing itself consisted of sleepers. All passengers, luggage, parcels, mail, etc. had to cross the line in this manner. *"There were people crossing most of the time and often they had a man there to watch over them and give them warning because trains were moving about and vehicles were being shunted"*. Apparently, the brickwork on the up platform, opposite the booking office, still shows faint signs of the rebuilding when the crossing was abolished and the platform height adjusted. Not only was the crossing dangerous for those using it, but there could be a nasty drop for passengers leaving trains which had stopped over it. In theory this was not supposed to happen, as the crossing was midway along the platforms and trains were generally so short that they only needed half the platform length at most. Nevertheless, the Health & Safety Executive would be most unhappy about such arrangements today!

Every time Ted Clissold visited Shrub Hill as a boy he was intrigued by the sight of the shunting horse. There were two Shire horses stabled at the station, one of which was generally on duty, with collar and harness, to move single vans, as required, often detached from one passenger train and attached to another. Between duties, the horse would be left to stand in the 'six foot' between the tracks and there, *"it would hardly move an ear, is would stand dead still"*, even with trains moving on either side.

By the time Ted Clissold came to work at Shrub Hill in 1918, the crossing had been replaced by a footbridge and the horses had given way to a shunting engine. There was still plenty of evidence that this was a joint station. The staff wore what, to all appearances, were Great Western uniforms, but the collar and cap initials were 'WJS', for Worcester Joint Station. There was no stationmaster as such, but a Joint Station Superintendent. His offices were at the foot of the stairs on the down platform. The Great Western Divisional Superintendent had his offices at the top of the same set of stairs - and there was some rivalry between the two. The Joint Station Superintendent wore a dark suit instead of a uniform. A GWR man in this post was supposed to be followed by a Midland man, and vice versa.

For several months early in his railway career, Ted worked in the inspector's office because they needed an assistant to assist the assistant inspector! In other words, he had to do the jobs that nobody else was willing to do although, unlike many railwaymen, he worked regular hours, finishing each day at 4.30pm in time to catch the 4.40 to Norton Junction. He had to distribute copies of important documents within the station area, for which there was even a primitive form of 'photocopier'. This was known as the 'jellypad' and involved a special jelly, which was boiled and poured into a frame the same size as a standard piece of paper. When it was cold and had set, the letter to be copied, which had been written in special ink, was placed face downwards and wiped over several times by hand. Subsequent sheets of paper placed on the jellypad and wiped over would produce copies. This worked for about eight or ten copies, after which the jelly would have to be boiled again.

Ted remembers rummaging around in the boiler house one day, near the signal box on the down platform. Here he found some old foot warmers - metal hot water bottles - which had not been used for many years. About twelve inches long and three inches deep, they had a stopper through which boiling water could be poured, a way of keeping passengers warm before compartments were heated by steam from the locomotive.

A Shrub Hill station staff photo taken in the early 1920's, the following are known:- Seated on the bench left to right, R W Higgins, Assistant Divisional Superintendent - Arthur Cope, Joint Station Superintendent- W.E Hart (with walking stick) Divisional Superintendent for GWR. Front row standing, extreme left is Inspector Garderner & next to him is Inspector Francis.

(Photo: Courtesy of Edward Clissold)

Shrub Hill station taken from the inside showing the footbridge, & the station crossing with a shunting horse stood on it. This picture is dated 1913. (Photo: Courtesy of Worcester Evening News)

Next to the boiler house was the lamp room, the base for lamp men who were employed to place lamps at the head and rear end of trains, to ensure that they were properly lit and that each train was displaying the correct headcode. More visible to ordinary passengers was their work within the station as darkness approached. They had a special torch, containing methylated spirits, with a protruding wick. They entered each compartment of a train standing at the station, undid the hinged glass lamp dome in the ceiling, lit the gas and put the dome back, locking it with a key. This was time consuming, especially if the train was already running late. Later there were pilot lights - known as 'by passes' - fitted to the gas burners. There was a master switch in each carriage, so that the whole carriage could be lit with a flick of this one switch.

Every September there was an influx of hundreds of hop pickers from the Black Country and South Wales. The oldest carriages were used for their trains and the pickers often arrived carrying such luggage they had for the fortnight in old tin boxes. Travelling in compartments labelled 'Hop Pickers Only', their main destinations were Bransford Road, Ashperton, Stoke Edith and Withington on the Hereford line, and Leigh Court, Knightwick and Suckley on the Bromyard line. Used to grim industrial surroundings for the rest of the year, most pickers brought their families with them and regarded their hard work in the fields as a paid holiday. When the farmer paid them at the end of the harvest, some immediately visited the nearest pub and *"they would have had rather too much to drink and you couldn't get them in the train"*......

Jim Beechey's first memories of Shrub Hill station also date from childhood. His grandfather, Tom Beechey, worked in the cloakroom and left luggage office for about 45 years, retiring in the early 1920s with a 'testimonial collection' amounting to about £50, an enormous sum in those days and a sign of the considerable affection and respect which fellow employees and regular passengers had for him. Around 1918, aged ten, Jim lived in Stanley Road. He used to take a meal up to his grandfather at the station, walking up Tallow Hill with sandwiches and a billycan full of tea. *"He used to work long hours and I often took another snack up at teatime"*, recalled Jim, so he may well have worked twelve hour shifts prior to the 1919 National Agreement, after which the eight hour shift became the norm. Tom Beechey was a founder member of the Worcester branch of the Railway Mission, which had buildings in East Street.

Although Jim never worked on the railway, some journeys from Shrub Hill still hold fond memories for him. On leaving school he went to work for Fownes, the glove manufacturers - Fownes Hotel on the City Walls Road is part of their former Talbot Street factory. During the summer of 1924 there was a works outing to the British Empire Exhibition at Wembley, a site which included the new football stadium. Fownes' chartered a special train, which ran on Saturday 21st June. It left Shrub Hill at 05.15, arriving in Paddington at 08.02. The return service did not leave Paddington until 12.40am on the Sunday morning. The handbill, still in Jim

Beechey's possession, advised passengers of the sights they could see in central London, as the exhibition did not open until 10am. Travel directions within London and to the exhibition referred to the Metropolitan Railway and the District Railway - they would not be known as underground 'lines' until they became part of the capital's integrated transport system on the formation of London Transport in 1933. Excursion passengers were also informed that, *"The train stops at Oxford on the outward and homeward journeys and a stop is also made at Charlbury to pick up passengers and no one should leave the train at this station"*. The area around Charlbury was where many of Fownes' home based outworkers lived. This is still fondly remembered by Jim Beechey as a very good day out, enjoyed by himself and his friends, especially as Fownes paid for the rail trip and the entrance fee to the exhibition.

As a young boy Jim joined the choir of Holy Trinity Church, next to the Vinegar Branch, and he remained a member of that choir for over forty years. The strong family interest in music meant that in the early 1930s he and his two brothers, plus two friends, formed a dance band - R.Beechey and his Dominion Dance Band. Early engagements were all in Worcester, but then they were invited to play at a Saturday night dance at Stoke Works. Having as yet no transport of their own they took the train from Shrub Hill, together with instruments, full drum kit and folding music stands. Fortunately the dance was at the salt works, next to the station, and it finished at 11.30pm, convenient for the last train back to Worcester. (The 1932 time-table shows a departure from Stoke Works at 11.54, arriving at Shrub Hill at ten minutes past midnight). The band completed several engagements there before they invested in their own transport. On one occasion some band members missed the train, so they left their instruments n the hall and walked to Droitwich where they borrowed bikes from friends living there to complete their journey. Why did they miss the train? - *"that was on account of the girls who had been at the dance you see, so we got delayed"*. As the band was offered more engagements out of town, their own transport became essential, so one of Jim's brothers bought a new Ford 8, plus a trailer, which took all five band members and their instruments......

Albert Baylis left school and joined the GWR, aged fourteen, in 1942. His first job was as a van boy, assisting on the railway-owned vehicles, collecting and delivering luggage and parcels within the city. After about six weeks, *"there was an opportunity I really jumped at, to enter Tunnel Junction Signal Box as a lad assistant to one of the signalmen"*. There were three such lads, they learnt a lot and had a great deal of fun. The signalmen, as was usual, took great pride in keeping the box clean. The signal levers were spotless, *"and woe betide anyone who used a lever without a duster and left his fingerprints behind"*. The floor had to be cleaned once a week until the linoleum shone, and the windows received the same treatment. Wartime workings past the box included ambulance trains returning empty stock to the south coast ports. They had priority over other trains and were distinguished by the huge red crosses on the sides and roof of each carriage.

In 1943 the need arose for a boy to help the platform inspectors at Shrub Hill - *"There were three inspectors and I was the only boy and certain duties were created, I suspect, just to keep me busy, like reading the gas meter every morning".* Other duties included handing passenger guards their wages envelopes at the end of each week, pinning up notices on the board and, accompanied by a member of the booking office staff, emptying the pennies from the slot machines on the toilet doors.

Albert was normally on the platform when the most important passenger train of the day arrived, the 08.55 to Paddington. The Hereford portion came in first, generally four coaches hauled by a 'Manor' or 'Hall', running right to the London end of the platform. The loco detached and went to the shed. The five coach Wolverhampton portion arrived a few minutes later, stopping short at the scissor crossing midway along the platform. The loco detached, drew forward and ran back over the scissors and crossover and went away to shed. The 'Castle' that was to haul the train to Paddington had been patiently waiting on another up road. It reversed on to the Hereford portion, which it propelled back onto the Wolverhampton coaches to unite the train. (The time-table confirms that this train left Hereford at 07.25, while the other portion left Wolverhampton at 07.00 and called at all stations to Worcester!). Even during the war, the loco for the 8.55 was kept as clean as conditions would allow, and every effort was made to run to time. As this train was being prepared for departure on 6th June 1944 someone called out, *"They've invaded, D Day is here!"*, causing a wave of excitement to sweep through the whole station.

Wartime or not, the racing pigeon fanciers of the Black Country continued with their hobby, many baskets of pigeons arriving on several trains within a short time, all to be released together at the appointed hour. The baskets were stacked in goods vans in the yard south of the station, all van doors open. The pin securing each basket's side opening was attached to string (more a 'network of string' than just a piece of string) and, when the time arrived, Albert had to pull the strings, which released the pins and freed hundreds of pigeons simultaneously, all circling in a great cloud above the station before dispersing.

After the war, disenchanted with the limited prospects that signalling seemed to offer - not all boxes were as interesting as Tunnel Junction - Albert left the railway, fulfiling a boyhood ambition to become an electrician. However, he returned, as a railway electrician based at Shrub Hill. He was responsible for maintaining the Lancing Bagnell electric vehicles used within the station, for pulling small trailers loaded with parcels etc. The driver of these once familiar machines stood on a small platform at the front. Albert Bayliss was also responsible for the diesel electric cranes used within the goods yards. They did not run on rails but were like small lorries, fitted with a jib. There were electric pumps at Pitchcroft, which drew water up from the Severn to Shrub Hill, where it was stored in large underground tanks, for use by engines on shed. These pumps were in Albert's care, as were the pumps at Charlbury which supplied the water troughs there. After a few years he left the railway and joined the staff of Worcester Technical College. Many years later, on a group visit to a signal box, he surprised the other members of the group, who were all younger than him, by the ease with which he operated one of the more difficult signals, a hard pull because of the considerable length of wire attached. He had not forgotten the technique, learnt from his days in Tunnel Junction Box - *"release the clip, lean on the lever, don't try to pull it, throw yourself backwards and when your weight is travelling you just straighten your arms and the momentum will pull the lever for you"* .....

Trevor Lettice has spent his railway career based at Shrub Hill station, beginning in 1957. For over forty years he has witnessed many changes, both to the station and its train services. When he remembered the former uses to which some areas had been put - during a guided tour he gave me one cold February evening in 2000 - it began to resemble a tour of a historic building rather than a working station. As with most historic buildings there is a resident ghost, or at least rumours of one. He even has a name, Harry, and is said to haunt the mail bridge linking the platforms, even though it has not been used for some years. There is, so they say, another ghostly figure who roams about the shed area, and a third who can sometimes be heard whistling down in the old goods yard.

My tour began at the north end of the station, on the down platform, looking towards Birmingham. Here was the site of the bay platform, filled in and topped with tarmac, the so-called 'Leominster Bay', from which trains for Bromyard, Leominster (and sometimes Hereford) departed. The Bromyard service was sparse and the bay was occupied by parcels vans for much of the day. Nearby, six 3-ton lorries were garaged beneath the station, their sole purpose was to distribute parcels brought in by passenger train. Post Office road vehicles waited 'in attendance' near the bay when a mail train was due. In one corner of the site there had been a group of lockers for Worcester's passenger train guards. Alterations to the wall brickwork is the only sign of a 'cupboard'. Shrub Hill had an allocation of three electric tugs (as they were known), used for pulling the once familiar trains of loaded trolleys along the platforms - each tug parked in turn at the 'cupboard' from where its batteries were recharged. The late types of trolleys, first seen in the 1960s, were known as 'BRUTES' - British Rail Universal Trolley Equipment - and the station had its own repair shop for these vehicles.

Moving along the down platform, the present day disabled toilet was once the busy office where railway staff, except goods yard workers, clocked on and off at the beginning and end of every shift. Today the station is closed only between 00.30 and 04.30, but then it was open for 24 hours a day. For many years a Leeds-Bristol train called around midnight and the Newcastle-Bristol mail called at 02.40. This train also carried passengers, many of them servicemen, so the ticket office and barrier were manned. The parcels office was open all night too and the station was a hive of activity in the small hours, with mailbags piled high on the platforms amidst the constant movement of trolleys. Some of the brickwork still bears the marks of persistent accidental 'Brute bashing'. Wooden skirting near the base of vulnerable sections of wall was fixed there in an attempt to reduce such damage. A steel post was positioned on the down platform, near the footbridge, in the hope that recklessly driven Brute would crash into it, rather than the flimsy looking Godfrey Davies car hire cabin next to it. Brutes tended to be taken across the lines on the crossing at the north end, because negotiating the goods bridge, with its lifts, meant opening and closing various sets of gates no fewer than sixteen times.

There was a cash office on the down platform, where four cashiers were seated at one large desk, counting and bagging cash from ticket receipts at other local stations, which had arrived in portable safes by train. There was a large safe in this office. Two other features of this platform, both long since vanished, were the first class ladies' waiting room, which was staffed by an attendant between 6am and 4pm, and the enginemen's cabin, with space for about ten train crew.

The ticket office was always open and the ticket barriers manned to ensure that no one strayed onto the platforms without a valid ticket. The Wymans Bookstall was almost under the footbridge, as was an office containing the railway's internal telephone switchboard for the whole Worcester area, which needed to be staffed by four telephonists. Nearby was the telegraph office, from which passengers could send telegrams. Whenever a heavy train en route to the Lickey Incline passed through, a message was sent via this office to Bromsgrove, informing them of the train weight and the number of banking engines required.

The left luggage and parcels office, with halved doors and a shelf on the lower half, is now bricked in. A little way along was the 'fish house', into which fish was unloaded from trains before being put onto lorries for delivery to its final destination. Fish arrived early in the morning, with vans from Grimsby and/or Hull detached from freight trains - *"If we had a fish job we used to put on our old uniforms for it; you also wore wellies and none of your mates would want to come near you afterwards, for obvious reasons"*.

The porters' room had several old style candlestick phones on the wall, connected to the signal boxes and shunters' cabins in the yard. The down platform signal box had been replaced by a bicycle shed. Nearby was the carriage examiner's office, and the lamp room, employing one man whose duty it was to change to change tail lamps of trains within the station area. There was also a shunters' cabin at this end of the station, added after Trevor arrived in 1957, because at that time they were still having to make do with two old guard's vans in a nearby siding. The bay at the south end of the down platform was used mostly for general parcels vans. Unlike the Leominster bay it was never used by passenger trains, with the exception of the Motorail service, which ran between Worcester and St.Austell for a few brief years in the 1970s.

The most prominent feature on the up platform is the curious building with attractive tiling and curved arch windows. During the 1940s it was a refreshment room, but had become an inspector's office by 1957. There has been much speculation as to its origins. It is said to have come from the first station to serve Worcester, at Spetchley, and moved here some time after Shrub Hill opened. Whilst the tiling is unique, the size and proportions of the windows, especially the round arches, certainly appear the same as those of other wayside stations built during the 1840s between Birmingham and Gloucester, including the original buildings at Kings Norton, erected in 1849.

Whatever the origins of this tiled building, one 1950s train invariably stopped alongside it. This was the late night Saturday 'dance special', an ex-Great Western railcar, which ran from Great Malvern through to Honeybourne. Arriving at Shrub Hill around 11.15pm, it was always crammed with young people in party mood. Railway workers had earlier discovered that ex-GW railcars could easily be rocked quite vigorously from side to side when standing at a platform - this they often did to the 'dance special', no doubt adding to the atmosphere within!

Other trains could be lively, even during the middle of the night. Summer Saturdays not only saw considerable holiday traffic during the day, but the overnight mail could have a surprising number of holidaymakers beginning their long trek to Ireland. It was also the mail's habit, on occasion, to disgorge large numbers of servicemen. Nobody had told Trevor about this and one night he was running up the footbridge steps, on urgent business, just as the mail drew to a halt - *"I rushed up the stairs and coming the other way was a load of squaddies, so I soon came back the same way again, virtually carried down"* ....

Finally, 'Tales of Shrub Hill' moves forward to the present day and out to the signal box at Norton Junction, which I visited courtesy of signallers David Pagett and Alan Gibson. The box is of standard Great Western design, with 15 levers in use. It controls train movements between Norton and Shrub Hill station, along the Cotswold Line to Evesham, and the short distance to Abbotswood, the junction with the original Birmingham & Gloucester main line. One unusual feature is a monitor screen on which the signaller can view train movements along this main line, even though they are controlled from the power box at Gloucester. The monitor is there for convenience, so that Norton can see which way Gloucester has set the points at Abbotswood for northbound trains - along the main line or towards Worcester. Main line signals are shown on the monitor simply as UM (up main) or DM if they are fully automatic but prefaced with a 'G' if they are not.

Norton's own distant signals are all colour lights. The distant on the approach from Shrub Hill is 1458 yards from the box, that from the Gloucester direction is 1033 yards, while the distant on the Cotswold Line, on the approach from Evesham, is

On the night of 26th February 1990 severe gales blew over Shrub Hill, the wind was so strong that all the Home signals at the north end of the station were bent round at right angles! This photo taken on the following morning shows the semaphores being replaced.

(Photo: Dave Gommersoll)

Table 14

Table 14

THE CATHEDRALS EXPRESS

RESTAURANT CAR SERVICE (¶)

LONDON, OXFORD
WORCESTER and HEREFORD

WEEK DAYS

		pm			am
London (Paddington)	dep	5A15	Hereford	dep	8A 0
Oxford	arr	6 27	Ledbury	„	8 21
Oxford	dep	6 35	Colwall	„	8 31
Kingham	arr	7 4	Malvern Wells	„	8 37
Moreton-In-Marsh	„	7 17	Great Malvern	„	8A42
Evesham	„	7 36	Malvern Link	„	8 46
Worcester (Shrub Hill)	„	7 55	Worcester (Foregate Street)	arr	8 55
			Worcester (Foregate Street)	dep	8 57
			Worcester (Shrub Hill)	arr	9 0
Fernhill Heath	arr	dd			
Droitwich Spa	„	8 19	Kidderminster	dep	8A34
Hartlebury	„	8 29	Droitwich Spa	„	8A48
Kidderminster	„	8 35			
			Worcester (Shrub Hill)	dep	9A10
Worcester (Shrub Hill)	dep	8 3	Evesham	„	9 30
Worcester (Foregate St)	„	8 7	Moreton-In-Marsh	„	9 55
Malvern Link	arr	8 17	Kingham	„	10 6
Great Malvern	„	8 20	Oxford	arr	10 33
Colwall	„	8 30	Oxford	dep	10 39
Ledbury	„	8 39	Reading General	arr	11 11
Hereford	„	8 59	London (Paddington)	arr	11 55

A—Seats can be reserved in advance on payment of a fee of 2s. 0d. per seat (see page 27).

dd—Calls to set down passengers on notice to the Guard.

¶—Restaurant Car available between London (Paddington) and Worcester (Shrub Hill), in each direction.

The "Cathedrals Express" timetable for September 1962 to June 1963.

Britannia class 4-6-2 No. 70013 "Oliver Cromwell" is seen at Shrub Hill on 19th August 1965, with an afternoon Paddington bound service.

(Photo: Bob Sim)

2453 yards away. In the days when all Norton's signals were manual the Cotswold Line distant, at least, would have been nearer the box, as a pull on this length and weight of wire would not have been possible. The home signal coming off the Cotswold Line is worked manually and, at 715 yards from the box, is a hard pull round a curve. An added feature of this curve is Saddlers Crossing, one of two farm crossings, with lineside phone, governed from the box.

Trains travelling from Norton to the Gloucester line have to pass Norton's No.10 signal, a standard Great Western type lower quadrant semaphore, the 'up main to branch home', 'main' in this sense being the Cotswold Line and the branch being the link to the Gloucester line. The lower arm on the same post is a semaphore distant signal (G126), controlled electronically from Gloucester when the line south is clear.

This is not the only mixture of old and new technology. Since most of the Cotswold Line was converted to single track in 1971, it has been worked by traditional single track token exchange apparatus. However, many passenger trains are not booked to stop at the box as tokens can also be exchanged at Shrub Hill. The track layout at Norton Junction was altered during singling. Trains from Evesham now have to travel 'wrong line' for a short distance before using the crossover near the box, which has a speed limit of just 30mph. In the early 1990s further detrimental alterations were planned. The double line between Norton and Shrub Hill station would become two single lines, in effect moving the junction back to Shrub Hill. It seemed as though nothing had been learned from the singling of the Cotswold and Hereford lines, and the clumsy layout through Foregate Street. Fortunately these most recent plans were never implemented.

The box at Norton Junction is, in the best railway tradition, spotless. It is open continuously, with four signallers covering three one man shifts by rota. During an average 24 hour period there are about sixty train movements through the junction. One of the most unusual is the 19.53 arrival at Shrub Hill from Gloucester, normally worked by a Class 153 single unit. This train started life as the 16.02 from Romsey, travelling via Southampton and Eastleigh. It is really several local services strung together for operational convenience. The train normally leaves Romsey as a three or four-car Sprinter, detached en route so that only the 153 works the whole service. There is no corresponding southbound train, the 153 returning only to Gloucester.

Plans to modernise the signalling in the Worcester area, possibly with a power box, seem unlikely to proceed. More recent thinking is that Worcester does not need its own power box, but can be controlled from Gloucester when that box needs renewal. In the meantime, the robustly built Worcester area boxes, a fascinating mixture of old and new, will continue, able to signal Worcester's increasing number of trains to a better future for many years to come.

John Boynton - April 2000

Ex LMS Jubilee class loco No. 45636 "Uganda", is seen approaching Shrub Hill, with a Saturday's only 'Down' Devonian, in the Summer of 1957. *(Photo: David Badham)*

The approach road to Shrub Hill station 1962. *(Photo: Martin Edgeworth collection)*

Photo taken from Sherriff Street level crossing, showing the Yard box. This photo was taken during a presentation for the best lorry driver of the year. Known persons in this picture are :-J Healey,S Ayres, A Hodges, W Rodway, A Bennett, W Webb,H King, W Evans, Tinkler, Petchey, A Parker, T Wooding, R Curnock, A Robinson,C Bevan & G Rivers.

(Photo: Courtesy of British Rail Worcester Archive's)

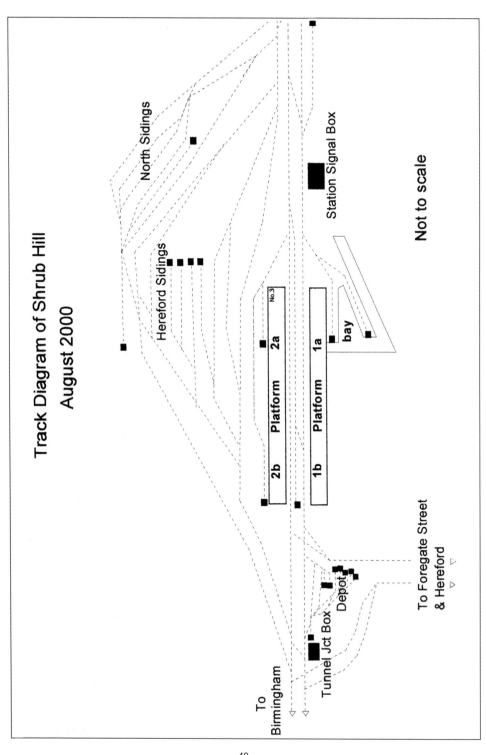

Track Diagram of Shrub Hill

August 2000

North Sidings

Hereford Sidings

Station Signal Box

Not to scale

Platform 2b Platform 2a No.3

Platform 1b Platform 1a

bay

To Birmingham

Tunnel Jct Box

Depot

To Foregate Street & Hereford

Significant Worcester Railway Dates

Date	Event
13th December 1824	A meeting is held at the White Lion, Bristol, where it is proposed to build a railway line to Birmingham via Gloucester, Tewkesbury and Worcester.
June 1835	Report in Worcester Journal said that the Birmingham/Gloucester railway project proposed to build a line a few miles east of Worcester.
25th September 1835	A joint meeting was held at the Star Hotel, Worcester, where the Birmingham Committee & the Gloucester Committee approved Capt Moorsom's plans, & the Birmingham & Gloucester Railway was conceived.
22nd April 1836	Birmingham & Gloucester Railway was incorporated by an Act of Parliament.
February 1837	Construction was underway of the Birmingham/Gloucester Railway.
26th June 1839	Worcester Chamber of Commerce establish a special committee to deal with the overriding important objective of putting the City of Worcester on the railway map. Its first concern was attempting to secure Worcester as a future station for the possible London/Dublin line. There were three possible routes, & the committee hoped that Brunel's idea, which was Didcot, Oxford, Worcester, Ludlow & Barmouth to finish at Port Dynllaen (now Portendynlleyn in North Wales) would be used. The other two routes did not go via Worcester. This plan failed in the end, together with another plan in 1846.
24th June 1840	Worcester's 1st Railway station is opened at Spetchley. A horse omnibus ran to & from the City to connect with the railway.The 1st train to arrive was a special, for opening the line from Cheltenham to Bromsgrove.
August 1841	The Directors of the Birmingham & Gloucester railway showed an interest in putting a line through the City of Worcester, however the Chamber of Commerce were to be disappointed again when the B&G proposed a branch line to Worcester instead of a through line. This branch line was to leave the main line at a new jct near

Tibberton, north of Warndon, & was to meet the Birmingham/Worcester canal, opposite St George's playing fields or near the present Royal Grammar School playing fields or close to the County Courts. The Chamber of Commerce did not agree to this & sent a special deputation to the B&G board proposing that the line should start at the then present Spetchley station & run to a terminus station at Sansome Fields, & that the running time between the stations should be no longer than 6 minutes. The B&G agreed the new route, but could not agree on the running times.

January 1844	Robert Stephenson opted for a branch line from near Spetchley to a terminus near the now Albion Inn, on the Bath Road, now A38. From this site there would be good access for the public & to Diglis basin.
19th March 1844	A meeting is held in the city at the Guildhall, & Mr F Elgie made a statement of the proposal by the Great Western Railway Co to construct what is now known as the Oxford, Worcester & Wolverhampton Rly, & requested support from the citizens to the scheme.
June 1844	Prospectus of the Oxford, Worcester & Wolverhampton Railway Company issued.
4th February 1845	The Railway Commissioners of the board of Trade reported in favour of the Tring line, & against the Oxford, Worcester & Wolverhampton line.
26th March 1845	The citizens of Worcester unanimously agreed to petition in favour of the Oxford, Worcester & Wolverhampton line, during another meeting.
4th August 1845	Her Majesty Queen Victoria gave Royal Assent to the Act of Parliament which incorporated the Oxford, Worcester & Wolverhampton Railway Company. The OWWR were empowered by this Act to build a railway from the Oxford Branch of the GWR to Evesham & Worcester to Grand Jct station at Wolverhampton, with branches to the river Severn ending at Diglis Basin. The Act also said that the railway was to be "constructed & completed in all respects to the satisfaction of the engineer for the time being to the Great Western Company", & "formed of such a gauge, & according to such mode of construction as will admit of the same being worked continuously with the said GWR ". Also

mixed gauge was to be provided on the northern section of the line from Wolverhampton to Abbotswood Jct, & also on the branch to Stoke Prior. This would allow the narrow gauge B&G trains to get to Worcester from both directions. The GWR was empowered to complete the line if the OWWR failed.

October 1845	The first general meeting of shareholders of OWWR was held in the Guildhall Worcester.
5th October 1850	Branch line opened off Birmingham/Gloucester line from Abbotswood to a station site at Shrub Hill. Norton Junction station opened. The line was worked by the Midland Company under a special agreement.
January 1851	Horse buses stop meeting the down mail train at Spetchley station.
18th February 1852	OWWR opened the Worcester to Droitwich line. Harbour Hill, becomes Tunnel Hill when the railway put a tunnel through it.
1st May 1852	The Official "First Train" to run over the OWWR proper, apart from Midland Trains from Abbotswood & Stoke Prior & various test trips, was a 21 carriage special, which left Stourbridge at 09.00 with cannon fire & church bells. The train reached Evesham just before noon, & according to the report 10,000 people had gathered to see the train. The special returned to Worcester Shrub Hill, where the Director's stopped for cakes & wine, which the Mayor of the city offered. The line was opened for normal traffic on the 3rd.
3rd May 1852	OWWR opened the line from Worcester to Evesham, also on this day the Droitwich to Stourbridge section of the line was opened.
July 1852	Norton Jct to Evesham section of line is doubled, & 52 acres of land situated to the north west of the station at Worcester is bought at a price of £8,500. After 1½ acres were sold, the remaining land was set aside as the site for the company's locomotive, carriage & wagon works.
1852	Four road terminal shed (goods) & three road through shed (passenger) opened (The 3 road passenger shed is rare due to the fact it was built on a curve.) Worcester Locomotive Works opened by OWWR

7th May 1853	Worcester was connected with Oxford. The line south from Evesham was single mixed gauge, however in several places the broad gauge line was incomplete, & the jct at Wolvercot had not been laid. A special train with 26 - four wheeled coaches being hauled by 2 loco's, made its way down the line passing Shrub Hill, which was still being built. At Evesham a champagne luncheon was provided before going on to Campden Tunnel with a special slow pass. When the train stopped at Wolvercot jct, the passengers had to walk on the ballast & cross the unfinished jct. The GWR had kindly laid on a connecting train to take them 4 miles to Oxford.
1853	A.C Sherriff (Alexander Clunes Sherriff) is appointed by the OW & W Rly as Shrub Hill Station master at the age of 40. He was a former schoolmaster, but had trained in railway management. With Shrub Hill under his control he started to get things happening, with traffic development, new lines being laid in the areas around Worcester. Worcester was fast becoming a really important railway centre. AC Sherriff was pensioned off when the GWR took over, He twice served as mayor of Worcester, & in 1865 became MP for the city. He held this position until his death in 1878.
1st October 1855	Worcester's 1st station, at Spetchley is closed to passengers, but continues as a goods station until 2nd Jan 1961. (Some special trains continued to serve Spetchley after closure, conveying excursion traffic to Spetchley Park.)
1858	Oxford, Worcester & Wolverhampton Railway experimented with continuous brakes for passenger trains, using Fay's & Newall's brake system. Various other makes/types of brake systems were tried, but in the end Sander's Automatic Vacuum, was modified to the present Great Western standard Automatic Vacuum brake in 1878. When the railway was being built westward towards Malvern part of the tunnel at Tunnel Hill was removed, thereby shortening the tunnel, & the soil was used for the great embankment across Sansome Fields to Foregate Street. The bridge over the canal near Rainbow Hill, was built with a hole in it, this was to reduce the weight of the brickwork & to save money.

25th July 1859	Henwick station opened, the first train departed at 8am, on a single line to Malvern Link, the small engine was decorated in evergreen leaves & flags, and given a real send off. A banner hung from a signal post which said "Hope, Peace & Plenty". There were 58 passengers & it took 15 minutes for the train to reach Malvern Link. Due to the Board of Trade inspector not passing the Severn Bridge fit for use, a train ran only from Henwick to Malvern Link. (In fact a brand new 2-2-2 locomotive from Stephenson's at Newcastle, plus some rolling stock was transported through the city street's & over the roadbridge from Shrub Hill, by horse & traction engines.)
17th May 1860	The original bridge over the River Severn is opened, together with the line to Malvern & Hereford, for the first two months trains leaving Worcester Shrub Hill, have to draw forward towards Birmingham, reversing at Tunnel jct, as the direct line from Shrub Hill to Foregate Street is not ready .The bridge over the Severn had not been built without problems before the Board of Trade inspector had found it unfit for use. The construction had been by Stephen Ballard of Colwall, & backed by Thomas Brassey a great railway constructor. The Viaduct & Bridge had a total length of 1½ miles, there are 68 arches, one of which, the Croft road bridge, was the first ever brick arch to be built on a skew. There was also a lot of trouble with the foundations. The two arches were cast iron, & it was a defect in one of the castings which the Board of Trade inspector noticed. Also the Butts branch is started, built towards Diglis. but only gets as far south as Dent's factory & Stallard's distillery,as the Cathedral chapter stop the line from running past the Cathedral.
1st July 1860	OWWR, becomes part of the West Midland Railway. (The directors of West Midland Railway took a deep interest in the welfare of its employees, & established a friendly society. This society known as The Railway Institute, was based at Shrub Hill station & was housed in the large rooms beneath the station. In front was a large area containing gardens, which had flowering plants. Also there was a Library in one of the rooms containing 3,000 books for self-education. The Institute made provision for its sick employees, as well as

arranging fetes & excursions.)

September 1861	Paddington becomes the London station for Worcester trains.
1st October 1861	Standard-gauge Paddington/Worcester service started, the average time for the 120 miles was 4hrs. (This was not improved for almost 30 years.)
1st August 1863	West Midland Railway is absorbed by Great Western Railway. Worcester Shrub Hill becomes a Midland/GWR joint station.
12th November 1864	West Midland Railway carriage works at Worcester are burnt down at night, with 18 new carriages destroyed in the fire.
1865	A number of executives of the old West Midland Rly established the Worcester Engineering Works Company, in order to build locomotives & rolling stock. The men concerned were Sherriff Thomas Rowley Hill & Walter Holland. After one good year, a slump caused problems, The company remained open only until 1871.
17th April 1868	Worcester Midlands Goods station, Goods Depot opens. 1870 Midland Engine Shed opens.
1872	The Lowesmoor Tramway opened, known as the Vinegar branch.This was a 900yd long private siding connecting the vinegar & cider works of Hill Evans & Co, with the main line near Worcester locomotive shed.
1875	Henwick box opened.
June 1882	The first service for the railway mission was held in the passenger guards room at Shrub Hill station. The services were especially arranged for railwaymen because of the long & irregular hours that they worked. The numbers attending grew & it was soon moved to the Workmans Hall near the centre of Worcester.In 1896 a mission Hall was built in East Street, Arboretum & was opened as a Railway Mission. This was used for 99 years.
1889	Shrub Hill Jct box & Foregate Street Station box opened.
1895	Loco No.3027 Achilles Class 7' 8" single is named "WORCESTER" withdrawn in 1914.

1894	Midland Engine Shed rebuilt (timber construction).
1896	During this time Worcester City was in the position of regularly receiving cattle & other livestock which needed to be taken to western side of the river. This caused a major problem, because Shrub Hill station was the only area large enough to unload the animals, when they would have to be walked through the city. It was decided to enlarge Henwick station so that the livestock could be unloaded nearer where they were needed.
July 1900	Worcester gets its 1st non-stop train from Paddington, the 120½ miles being covered in 2hrs 15 minutes for the down service, & the up Service 2hrs 20 minutes. This service was regular & continued to Hereford.
1905	Worcester Tunnel Jct box opens.
1906	River Severn Railway Bridge is rebuilt.
1909	Rainbow Hill Jct box opens.
May 1909	The Bridge over Foregate Street is replaced by a more elaborate bridge, towards which the city council denoted £162. This money went towards the curved arch & crests of the GWR & City, which can still be seen today.
1910-1913	The 1st footbridge is built at Shrub Hill station. Before this passengers had to use a foot crossing over the line to get to the other platform. This was roughly in the same position as the footbridge.
1916	Blackpole halt opened by GWR.
1919	Blackpole halt closed by GWR.
31st March 1924	Rushwick Halt & Boughton Halt opened by the GWR.
1927	Bulldog class loco No.3353 "Plymouth" is renamed "PERSHORE PLUM" on the 100th anniversary of the discovery of this plum. GWR Saint loco's are replaced by the GWR Star locos, on the Paddington,Birmingham,Wolverhampton via Shrub Hill.
1928	Part of the long shunt spur at Henwick is adapted to form a private siding for the Mining Engineering Company, this extended from the overbridge (122m 27½ ch) to the stop block at the Malvern end of the siding &

could hold up to 19 wagons. A gate was provided on the Worcester side of the overbridge. This needed to be kept closed except when the shunt entered. A white light was fixed to a post of the gate to mark the spot at night.

1930	A new siding is installed on the Butts Branch for horsebox traffic to the nearby racecourse.
1930	GWR & LMS ticket offices are replaced by one ticket office timber built in the middle of the station entrance. Auto-cars started in service at Worcester.
1931	The southernmost portion of the riverside branch closes.
August 1932	Bulldog class loco No. 3414 (A.H MILLS) is renamed "SIR EDWARD ELGAR".
12th December 1932	Midland Engine Shed closes 1935. The joint station signal box at Shrub Hill is rebuilt & repositioned. Castles start to work over the Cotswold line to Worcester.
July 1935	1st GWR railcar at Worcester No.7, followed by No.6 in August both new.
8th July 1935	A diesel GWR railcar service is introduced between Oxford/Worcester & Hereford.
1936	Shrub Hill is handling ¾ million parcels.
18th May 1936	Astwood Halt opens to coincide with the introduction of GWR railcars.
1938	185,000 tons of freight at Worcester, this included 10,000 tons of Tin cans, 8,000 tons of machinery, 5,000 tons of vinegar & 2,000 tons of Lea & Perrins sauce. Worcester received its first allocation of Castles Nos 5049,5050 & 5063.
c1938	Overall roof is taken off Shrub Hill Station.
1939	Midland Engine Shed demolished.
31st July 1939	During the 1930's some doubts were cast on the accuracy of the speed record achieved by "City of Truro" in 1904, however in 1939 the Great Western Rly attained a fully-authenticated 100mph maximum. "Builth Castle" No. 4086 was timed by R.E Charlewood at

	100mph at the foot of Campden Bank, near Honeybourne while at the head of 12:45 Paddington/Worcester Express. (Of course LNER "Mallard" had already managed 126mph while descending Stoke bank.).
25th September 1939	Astwood Halt closes.
October 1939	LNER J25 0-6-0 No's.1986,2061,2065 & 2075 arrived at Worcester shed on loan to GWR.
1940	Blackpole halt reopened by GWR.Due to the War, female guards employed on the trains at Shrub Hill.
1940	The last Birmingham / Bristol mail train is unloaded at Spetchley station, after which it runs via Shrub Hill.
March 1941	GWR Parcels railcar No.33 arrived at Worcester shed new. (To traffic May 1941).
1942	Due to the wartime traffic GWR lengthened & modified the 'up' refuge siding into a loop, at Henwick.
September 1943	USA 2-8-0 class S160 loco arrived to Worcester Shed No's 2270 & 2424.
1944	Coaling facilities improved & a coaling hoist added at Worcester shed A connection at Henwick is installed, worked by a ground frame to provide in the 'down' main line 12yds on the Worcester side of the level crossing, to the Worcester Corporation Power Station with 3 private sidings & own shunting loco. This cost the City of Worcester £1,519.
September 1944	USA 2-8-0 class S160 loco leave Worcester Shed No's 1628, 1660,1665, 1684, 2279, 2338, 2357, 2435, 2442 & 2443. WD 2-8-0 loco's arrive at Worcester Shed, No's 7043, 7148, 7229, 7233, 7243, 7400, 7404, 7418, 7458, 7464.
1946	Blackpole halt closed again, by GWR.
June 1946	Castle class No. 7005 new to Worcester shed from Swindon Works with the name "Lamphey Castle".
1947	Loco No.1029 "County Of Worcester" is outshopped from Swindon Works.
19th March 1947	Free emergency shuttle train service using a GWR

railcar from Henwick to Foregate St was run for four days only. This was due to the River Severn flooding when it rose 17ft above its normal level.

1st January 1948	British Railways is born (The name was changed to British Rail in the 1960's).
1949	Worcester Locomotive Works up graded to "factory" status.
1950	Auto-cars services withdrawn at Worcester.
1951	Worcester Locomotive Works down graded to "Loco concentration depot" status.
25th April 1953	Racehorse facilities were withdrawn, from the Butts branch. This was the last time this branch was used, the branch was worked by two LNER J25 0-6-0 loco's which were on loan to the GWR, Nos 1989 & 2040.
1955	The Butts branch ceased to be used Summer 1955. 100 passenger trains calling daily at Shrub Hill, including the "Devonian".
25th September 1955	Signal gantry over the tunnel on the signal box side of the tunnel removed.
1st February 1957	Butts branch officially closed & removed in the same year.
August 1957	Castle class loco No. 7005, (Lamphey Castle) is renamed "SIR EDWARD ELGAR" at the time of the centenary of the composer's birth. Also the "CATHEDRALS EXPRESS" first started running as 07:45. Hereford/Paddington, stopping only at Evesham & Moreton-in Marsh on its journey between Oxford & Worcester. (The two events are linked in with the Three Choirs Festival, which is held in Worcester this year.)
February 1958	The whole line to Bristol south-west of Barnt Green has now become part of the Western Region, having been part of the Midland Region until then. Bromsgrove is now a sub shed of Worcester (85A).
1958	Swindon-built "Cross-County" DMUs class 120's start to work the Birmingham Snow Hill - Worcester-Hereford-South Wales services. These new unit's are fitted with Miniature Buffets.

1959	Cotswold line sees its first Britannia class steam loco on the London services.
16th August 1959	Worcester Foregate Box closes.
7th September 1959	Norton Junction station is renamed Norton Halt.
1960	Worcester is handling 950 wagons on an average day.
May 1960	Worcester Locomotive Society formed.
1961	08.00 Birmingham/Carmarthen & return at 15.10 is the longest DMU working in the country, with a round trip of 384 miles.
31st May 1962	1st Western diesel No. D1000, "Western Enterprise" arrives at Worcester, on 10:15 stopping service from Wolverhampton to Worcester.
October 1962	WR tries 24hr clock, on timetables, posters at the start of the winter timetable.
October 1962	At the start of the winter timetable most of Worcester's remaining GWR Railcars are withdrawn & replaced by BR type single car units for use on the Bromyard branch & some local services. Kidderminster's GWR Railcars are also to be withdrawn. The vehicles have been condemned on the grounds of age & inefficient heating apparatus, which would be too expensive to replace. However two railcars are being retained at Worcester as reserves.It was not uncommon to find a parcels van attached at the rear of the DMU formation at this time. Railcars withdrawn at Worcester:- No's 20,22,23,24,26 & 32.
December 1962	The only normal express services into & out of Paddington which are still exclusively steam hauled are those to Oxford, Worcester & Hereford.These are chiefly covered by a Worcester "Castle", plus a few from Old Oak Common.However a Didcot "Hall" is not unknown.
1963	The Beeching Plan, published.
23rd Jan 1963	First diesel to arrive at Worcester for crew training. BRCW type 3 Loco No D6518 (33013). The class 33s loco's are used on the Fawley to Bromford Bridge, Esso oil tank trains.

24th April 1963	Worcester control office was disturbed to learn that 2-8-0 No.4705 was heading in its direction on a parcels train, as this class is barred beyond Oxford. They had it removed at Honeybourne in favour of a "Hall" class loco.
9th May 1963	Hymek D7076 arrives at Worcester for crew training, only 3 days old. Stayed until July 63. Also D7048 & D7078 are used on training on loan from Old Oak Common, plus another one from Cardiff.
May 1963	Hymeks start to work on the Worcester/Paddington's.
12th August 1963	For the first time, so far as it is known a Paddington - Worcester service was worked by a "Western" class diesel. D1068 "Western Reliance" headed the 11:15 Paddington - Worcester & returned to Paddington with 15:10 from Worcester, this was due to a Hymek failure.
7th September 1963	The Cotswold line was the last route to go to diesel from steam. Total dieselisation of the Paddington - Worcester - Hereford services was scheduled from the start of the winter timetable. The last rostered steam turn was that of "Castle" No. 7023 with 11:10 am Worcester - Paddington & 19:15 return. However as a result of diesel failures no fewer than 73 substitutions of steam for diesel traction were recorded in the first 3 weeks of the timetable on the Paddington - Worcester & Worcester - Hereford diagrams combined. The diesel diagrams include 2 night freights between Paddington - Worcester. Three of Worcester's "Castles" Nos. 7005, 7013 & 7025 were still active at the end of September. Also there were 7 express trains in both directions, including the "Cathedral Express" . Most trains were standardised at a quarter past alternate hours starting with 09:15 to Hereford. The "Cathedrals Express" still included its Kidderminster portion as a last reminder of the days OWWR Expresses ran to Wolverhampton. On the Worcester Shrub Hill / Hereford line there were six trains week days in each direction run at 10 minutes past alternate hours. Time taken 80 minutes on the 'down' & 83 minutes on the 'up'.
September 1963	Last scheduled Up steam "CATHEDRALS EXPRESS" from Worcester to Paddington, with loco 7005 "Sir Edward Elgar".

13th September 1964	Crew training starts with English Electric type 3 diesels (class 37's) No.s D6939, D6940, D6941 & D6942.
21st March 1964	The Paddington - Worcester line was used to individually evaluate a short list made from all the remaining "Castle" class locomotives. The service for the testing was 09.15 Paddington - Worcester SH and return 13.15 Worcester SH - Paddington. This was in connection with a final high speed run from Paddington to Plymouth & return on 9th May 1964. For example, 4079 Pendennis Castle was tested on 28th April, complete with GWR style number on the buffer beam & hauling the evening express back to Paddington. The other Castle's tested were 4079, 5054, 7008, 7022, 7023, 7025, 7029 & 7032. 7029 tested on 24th March, 4079 1st April , 7023 20th April and 7022 21st April.(The loco's which were used are 4079 Pad-Ply 7029 Ply-Bristol & 5054 Bristol-Pad).
16th May 1964	Oxford University Railway Society ran "CASTLE FAREWELL" tour using No.5054 "Earl of Ducie". Route was Paddington, Oxford, Worcester, Hereford Newport & back to Paddington via the Severn Tunnel.
5th June 1964	Last train on Vinegar Branch was hauled by loco 1639, & driven by Kenneth Matthews, with Edward Rowberry who was the district signal lampman, whose job it was to open & close the gates. (The line was closed in July of that year.)
12th July 1964	Steam loco .Peppercorn A1 Pacific No.60114 "W.P ALLEN" visits Worcester on a railtour run by The Derbyshire railway Society. Failed at Worcester with a bent rod, & stayed for one month, until returning north back to the eastern region.
August 1964	Crew training starts with Brush type 4's diesels (class 47's), 3 loco's at Worcester brand new from Brush Works D1613,D1614 & D1615. Stayed at Worcester until November 64.
4th September 1964	The last steam hauled local train from Birmingham Snow Hill to Worcester, hauled by a "County" class loco.
5th September 1964	Normal services to Bromyard ceased.
6th September 1964	Last train from Bromyard, hauled by Collett loco's Nos

	2232 & 2222. The special train was arranged by Bill Morris.
1st October 1964	Locomotive repair works closes.
October 1964	3 steam locos taken into Worcester Works, to be repainted and restored for private use on the Dart Valley Rly. Loco No's 1420, 6435 & 4555.
3rd/4th October 1964	Rail bridge installed over the northern link road at Blackpole.
29th October 1964	Worcester Railway Works closed.
17th November 1964	Castle class loco No. 7005 "Sir Edward Elgar", is withdrawn and denamed at Worcester depot.
1965	"CATHEDRALS EXPRESS" is denamed, this was due to the fact that the headboard would not fit on diesel locos. (The "Cathedrals Express" was the last scheduled steam hauled express to be hauled by Castle's). Gas works branch & Underwoods coal yard closed.
5th April 1965	Henwick Station, Rushwick Halt & Boughton Halt close, however freight traffic at Henwick continued.
June 1965	Building of Elgar House, office block in front of Shrub Hill Station commences. The new Summer Timetable introduced, saw the number of down expresses cut to six & only four trains conveyed portions for Hereford. Paddington departures remained at a quarter past the hour, but Shrub Hill departures were a mixture of 00.00, 00.25 & 0040. The Kidderminster portion ceased.
14th June 1965	Accelerated schedules on the Worcester/Paddington route. The Birmingham/Bristol line is scheduled for complete dieselisation, however several workings continued to be powered by steam.
8th August 1965	Special steam charter using GWR No.4079 "Pendennis Castle" Paddington, Oxford, Worcester, Gloucester, Swindon & Paddington.
December 1965	Engine sheds closed to steam (remained as a stabling point only). Last day of Steam at Worcester, Last loco in steam 0-6-0PT No. 3682, this loco belonged to Worcester depot.

2nd January 1966	Last "Jubilee" class loco to work to Shrub Hill, light engine from Abbotswood direction. Loco No.45697 "Achilles".
3rd January 1966	Norton halt is closed.
4th January 1966	Down platform to Down middle & Up middle to Up platform connections in centre of station abolished.
2nd February 1966	Crew training starts on Peak class diesels, No.D148 arrived from Bristol & stayed for one month.
Summer 1966	Steam Loco No. 47681 is cut up at Worcester. It was the only loco ever to be cut up at Worcester. The loco was being towed to the scrap yard at Cashmore's, Newport & while passing through Worcester developed a hot box. It was decided to destroy the loco where it was rather than repairing the fault.
August 1966	At least 8 months after the official end of steam on the Western region, & 3 years after the official withdrawal of the Castle's on the London services, Stanier class 5's & 8F's are still regularly seen at Shrub Hill.
1967	Western Region introduce the fastest ever timed Worcester - Paddington service, 2hrs 5mins. (07.50 Worcester - Evesham and Oxford, passengers from Moreton in Marsh - Kingham & Charlbury had to catch the 07.10 from Worcester & change at Oxford.). Plans to single the Cotswold line are made known.
18th April 1967	New freight & parcels concentration depot opened at Sheriff Street. Over a 1,000 tons of goods in full wagon loads & some 80,000 small items of general merchandise were handled each week at the depot, which served an area of over 1,000 square miles.
16th October 1967	BR's sheeting Works at Shrub Hill gutted by fire.
December 1967	The curved viaduct to the Butts branch is taken down.
c1968	Water pumping station by river pulled down.
1968	Blackpole Sidings box closed. First Diesel Hydraulic Warship loco to Worcester was D855 "Triumph", which came for crew training.
1st May 1968	Goods traffic at Henwick is withdrawn. (Handled coal

traffic 2nd Jan 1967 - 1st May 1968).

18th June 1968	Goods yard signal box closed. Up avoiding & Up goods lines made dead ended at Tunnel Jct end & direct access to London yard at Tunnel Jct taken out of use July 1968. From the beginning of the new timetable Worcester-Paddington trains have been worked by North British Warship class diesels & Brush type 4's.
4th August 1968	The Wagon Works complex taken out of use.
30th November 1968	Private Mining Engineering Co sidings traffic at Henwick withdrawn, and all connections except the main line crossovers were taken up late 1968, early 1969. The up goods loop was returned to its original refuge siding.
February 1969	Worcester's Railway Works demolished.
12th April 1969	Worcester's first open day, which was held on the stabling point. A Midland Blue Pullman was one of the main exhibit's car No's 60090, 60730, 60731, 60740, 60741 & 60091. Also on display were :- steam loco 7808 "Cookham Manor", plus diesel's, D165, D839, D856, D1038, D1614, D2177, D2183, D2184, D2185, D2190, D2193, D2195, D3964, D4118, D4120, D6321, D6324, D6325, D6329, D6342, D7007, D7009, D7050, D7061, D7100.
13th June 1970	Worcester Shrub Hill to Bristol TM and Newton Abbot Motorail service began.
13th July 1969	Four road terminal shed (goods) is demolished at Worcester depot.
1971	The Worcester/Oxford line is singled from Norton Jct, this saw the end to regular freight traffic on the line. 28.75 miles of line from Worcester to Moreton will be singled, leaving a passing loop at Evesham. Next came news that 13.75 mile line from Wolvercot jct to Ascott-under-Wychwood would be reduced to a single line. Also semi-fast trains from Birmingham/Worcester & Hereford via Kidderminster are withdrawn.
October 1971	Diesel Hydraulic loco D844 "Spartan", used as a temporary train heating boiler at Shrub Hill, until November 71.
28th November 1971	The level crossing gates at Henwick are replaced by full

The first class 150 Sprinter unit, No. 150001, is seen for the first time at Shrub Hill station on the day of its launch. In the pouring rain on 21st January 1985. These units took over from the DMU's.(Local railway staff have nicked named this unit "SCUD") *(Photo: Denise Johnson)*

The last weekday loco hauled "Cathedrals Express" 18:07 Paddington-Hereford, is seen leaving Shrub Hill on 8th May 1987, with Class 50 loco No. 50033 "Glorious". *(Photo: Stephen Widdowson)*

lifting barriers.

19th December 1971	Rainbow Hill Jct to Tunnel Jct singled. New facing connection up loop to down loop on Tunnel Jct side of the Rainbow Hill Jct points. Trains towards Hereford regained their proper line by a crossover Foregate Street side of the Jct.
1972	Resignalling scheme was proposed, which would have bought coloured light signalling to Worcester, & closed 4 signal boxes. However this did not take place.
6th May 1972	Motorail service starts from Shrub Hill, 07:00 to Totnes (10.40) and St Austell (12.50) then on to Penzance. The return service left Penzance at 15.40, then to St Austell (16.35) where the 1st lot of car flats are attached, Totnes (18.20), arriving back at Shrub Hill 22.10. This service only ran during the summer timetable
December 1972	Tolladine bridge, next to the railway club, is strengthened.
c1973	Telegraph office closes at Shrub Hill. T.O.P.S started on the Western Region.
May 1973	Class 31's to take over from Hymeks on the London service However the class 31's were not up to the Express work on the London service's. Campden bank on a damp day caused problems for these locos, and during November 73, Pilot locos had to be attached to assist the train as for as Moreton in Marsh the pilot loco would be a class 37 or 25.
19th May 1973	9F 2-10-0 "Black Prince" worked over Cotswold line, with a tour by the Wirral Railway Circle. via Shrub Hill & on to Hereford.
24th June 1973	6998 "Burton Agnes Hall" on a GWS special, via Foregate St & Shrub Hill, towed away from Shrub Hill with a Peak class diesel over Cotswold line.
6th May 1973	Diesel depot closes at Shrub Hill.
9th June 1973	The double line in the middle road of the station is converted into a single line.
September 1973	Wylds Lane signal box closed, & new ground frames installed at North sidings & Midland yard.

22nd September 1973	Hymek No.'s D7001 & D7028, pass through Shrub Hill with the Western Region "Hymek Commemorative" rail tour.
1st October 1973	British Rail Catering, have taken the new name of Travellers-Fare, for both train services & stations.
October 1973	The double line between Rainbow Hill Jct & Henwick via Foregate Street converted to two single lines. The former up line became to/from Tunnel Jct only, while the former down line was to/from Shrub Hill only.
14th October 1973	A new 40mph crossover from up main to down main was installed at Henwick. A week later a new facing Jct was installed between Rainbow Hill and Shrub Hill Jct.
November 1973	Shrub Hill Jct Box & Rainbow Hill Box close.
December 1973	North bay filled in at Shrub Hill Station.
January 1976	English Electric class 50 diesel locos 50025 & 50047 arrive at Worcester from Bristol for crew training.
3rd January 1976	D1055 "Western Advocate" collided with the rear of the Curzon Street/Worcester SH parcels train which was being hauled by loco 31240,near the north side of Worcester tunnel.
16th March 1976	50021 reported on 14:00 Worcester SH/Paddington - one of the first class 50's on the Cotswold line.
Early 1976	The midday train from Paddington / Worcester SH (arr 12.30) is a pair of locos. The extra loco usually a class 52 Western diesel, which would be attached to the front of the train at Oxford, which was normally a class 47. This pair 47+ 52 then worked to Shrub Hill. The class 52 would then be taken off & would pick up a scrap metal train, which had come up early from Birds Scrap Company at Long Marston. This train was then taken over the Cotswold line to Temple Mills yd, London .
June 1976	Last Post Office mail vans in the south dock at Shrub Hill.
January 1977	Western diesel loco D1023 "Western Fusilier", works a special charter (CAPITALS UTD EXPRESS) via Worcester Foregate Street & Shrub Hill, from Paddington to Hereford via Bristol, then Hereford to

Paddington.

May 1977	Protoype HST coaching stock is stored at Worcester Depot, car No.s. 41000, 41002, 42002, 40000 & 40500. Stayed at the depot until November 77.
14th May 1977	Class 24 loco No. 24142 - (TDB968009) Train heating unit arrived at Worcester, moved to Oxford during 1978.
1978	A new travel centre & telephone enquiry complex is built at Foregate Street station.
29th January 1978	RPPR special charter "Deltic Dragon" using Deltic diesel No.55018 "Ballymoss" over the Cotswold line to Shrub Hill. Then on to Gloucester and Newport.
11th March 1978	The Cotswold Line Promotion Group is formed, to safe guard the Worcester/Oxford line.
23rd September 1978	The last Motorail service leaves Shrub Hill, to St Austell headed by class 50 diesel loco 50044 "Exeter", which also worked the last return service the same day.
Late 1970's	Steam heating carriage units, ceased being used. There is one in Midland yard, & one in the station area. (Steam pipes can still be seen on the far side of platform two, they ran to the middle road.)
12th July 1981	Merrymaker trip starting at Shrub Hill to Plymouth & Newquay price £5.70.
28th November 1981	Deltic diesel No. 55022 "ROYAL SCOTS GREY" stops at Shrub Hill, with "DELTIC VENTURER" charter.
May 1982	BR set out plans to withdraw all through main line train services between Paddington, Worcester & Hereford, due to the poor condition of the track, & the fact that it needed £1.5 million spent on repairs.
15th May 1982	The last loco hauled 15.15 Paddington/Worcester SH. Hauled by class 50 No. 50033, which carried a "Cathedrals Express" headboard for the day
May 1983	Long term improvements on the Birmingham/Hereford passenger service began. Worcester ticket receipts increased by over 300% in less than 6 months.
25th February 1984	Class 50 loco 50007 "Hercules", is renamed "Sir

Edward Elgar" at Paddington station, to mark 50th anniversary of the composer's death.

March c1984	Platform ticket machine taken out of use, when station was made an open station.
6th April 1984	First class 58 diesel loco passes through Shrub Hill yard on a crew training trip to/from Bescot. (58010).
26th April 1984	Diesel class 25 No. 25176, hauls diesel loco's 27002, 27019, 08570 and 27036 through Shrub Hill from Scotland to Swindon Wks.
14th May 1984	1st High Speed Train service from Paddington to Worcester & on to Gt. Malvern, power car No's 43133 & 43134, & the launch of the "Cotswold & Malvern Express". The new HST service showed a net revenue growth of 11.3%, compared with the DMUs which ran in the same path.
October 1984	Worcester Foregate railway bridge is painted green. It was battleship grey before.
30th November 1984	0705 Hereford/Paddington (1A20) is derailed at Stoulton near milepost 115. The train which is being hauled by loco 47500 "Great Western" is split in half leaving the last three carriages against the farm bridge, while the rest of the train stops just past the site of Stoulton station. No major injuries, a broken fish plate is blamed as the cause.
21st January 1985	First class 150 sprinter to arrive for publicity/media launch at Shrub Hill. (Unit No. 150001).
February 1985	Class 84 Electric Loco's No's 84004 & 84005 arrive from Crewe, stored in yard, then on to Birds for scrap at Long Marston.
13th May 1985	"CATHEDRALS EXPRESS" is re-launched, using the 07.05 Hereford/Paddington service, loco 47627 "City Of Oxford" was at the head of the 1st train.
4th September 1985	Loco No. 47607 is named "ROYAL WORCESTER" at Worcester Foregate Street station as part of GWR 150 celebrations by Councillor Poole & Mr R.T George Divisional Manager of Royal Worcester Spode Ltd. The special GWR 150 exhibition train was at Foregate station for 3 days.

10th December 1985	Travellers Fare Chief Steward Alex Frost of Worcester, awarded with MBE on board an Inter-City Train, by Lord Lieutenant, Hereford & Worcester, Thomas Dunn.
16th January 1987	Due to changes in the postal distribution system, Worcester loses its Travelling Post Office trains. Last train northbound 1M36 hauled by loco 45149, & last train south bound service 1V97 hauled by loco 45115.
3rd April 1987	The track has started to be lifted from the rest of Midland yard. The Wylds Lane Trading Estate has just been built.
8th May 1987	The last weekday loco hauled "Cathedrals Express" 18:07 Paddington/Hereford, replacement by new HST Diesel Class 50 No. 50033 "Glorious" at the head of the train.
11th May 1987	First weekday for the Cathedrals Express as an HST, using power cars No's 43017 & 43032.
20th September 1987	First class 155 Sprinter at Worcester for Crew training Unit no. 155303.
28th February 1988	Worcester Midlands Goods station, Goods Depot taken out of use.
6th May 1988	The first class 59 diesel loco passes through Shrub Hill on its way to Severn Valley Diesel Gala. (59001 Yeoman Endeavour).
June 1988	Worcestershire County Council is interested in the possibility of a multi-million pound station & inland port warehousing terminal for use with the channel tunnel project,at the point where the Worcester/Oxford line crosses the Birmingham/Bristol line, near Abbotswood Jct.
July 1988	Newspaper train service withdrawn from Worcester. Deliveries by road preferred.
8th October 1988	During the weekend of 8th - 10th October, an 800 ton rail bridge was pushed into place over the new southern link road. The bridge was built along side the railway, then the embankment was dug away. The bridge was then pushed 50 yards (taking taking 5hrs), into its resting place. The complete job took only 46hrs until trains were running over it.

14th January 1989	Class 156 sprinter units start to work the Cardiff services from Worcester.
October 1989	2nd week in October MAS aspect signal is installed next to Metal Box, followed by a MAS signal at Norton Jct. 10th November 1989. Her Majesty the Queen & HRH Duke of Edinburgh, arrive at Shrub Hill station on the Royal Train, which is hauled by Loco 47821 "Royal Worcester". Her Majesty names loco 47528 "The Queen's Own Mercian Yeomanry" in the south dock at the station.
3rd December 1989	The last remaining shed at Worcester depot (3 road Passenger) is pulled down.
End 1989-start 1990	Signal moved at North end of Shrub Hill Station, due to it being the wrong side of the crossing (26th February 1990). Semaphore signals at the north end of Shrub Hill are bent at right angles, due to overnight gales.
28th March 1990	The first Class 158 unit to arrive at Worcester, for testing in the area. (158704).
April 1990	A new fueling point is built on the site of the 3 road passenger shed.
18th September 1990	Washer plant is installed at the depot.
28th March 1991	Fuel tanks are installed on the depot.
April 1991	New county council pressure is being put on BR to establish an out of town Parkway station at Norton to provide an Inter-city link-up. The lengthy delay in the resignalling scheme has ensured the survival of Norton Jct box & its semaphore signalling for some time to come. Crew training on class 158 units at Worcester starts. (158752).
8th July 1991	09001 arrives at Worcester, for use for shunting Metal Box & MoD Long Marston traffic. Left Worcester on 2nd August, when it went for display at Gloucester open day, never returned.
1992	Worcester's first female driver Barbara Bowes.
May 1993	Introduction of Turbo units from Worcester to Oxford & Paddington. First class 165, 165137 & 1st class 166, 166203.

2nd May 1993	Worcester Rail Open Day, held in the yard at Shrub Hill Loco 37185 is named "Lea & Perrins", and Loco 37114 is named "City of Worcester" at Shrub Hill station.
16th May 1993	The last timetabled loco hauled service from Paddington to Worcester. 15:37 Sundays only Paddington/Worcester, was hauled by loco 47821 "Royal Worcester" and carried a Cathedrals Express headboard. The services now use Turbo's or HST's.
22nd August 1993	The first time a GWR King class loco has been into Worcester No. 6024 was driven by Jack Saunders & Fireman Robin Hancox.
December 1993	The cutting on the signal box side of the tunnel, is taken back and terraced to stop landslips, which it has been prone to over the last 4 years.
7th March 1994	Platform Nos at Shrub Hill are changed. Platform 1 was the north bay, this was filled in, in the 70's. Therefore Shrub Hill did not have a platform 1, the numbers of the platform's were 2 & 3, then over the footbridge to 4 and 5. Platform 6 was the far bay. Now the platforms are 1a and 1b - 2a and 2b-3.
26th March 1994	Class 50 diesel, No 50007 "Sir Edward Elgar" is withdrawn at midnight at Paddington station, having worked the last ever class 50 hauled train on BR. The loco has since been purchased, & is now at the Midland Railway Centre.
April 1994	BR is privatised, Shrub Hill station is now owned by Railtrack, who lease the station to Central Trains.
22nd May 1994	Worcester Rail Festival, held in the yard at Shrub Hill.
June 1994	New class 92 electric loco No. 92009, is released from Brush Works, Loughborough with the name "Elgar".
15th April 1997	Refurbished clocks at Worcester Shrub Hill station, believed to be 70-100 years old are now electronic, but did not go digital ! due to station being a Grade 2 listed building and Railtracks pledge to preserve its heritage. Clocks put back up at station on 15/4/97. When being refurbished a brass plaque was found inside one of the clocks showing the date of 1909 written on it.
27th September 1997	"CATHEDRALS EXPRESS" is denamed.

22nd May 1998	The Midday "Cotswold & Malvern Express", last day running for an HST formation (43128-43129). Will be a class 166 Turbo from 25th May.
2nd September 1998	First Class 66 diesel loco through Shrub Hill, No. 66004, Newport Bescot.
11th September 1998	All signal lamps at Shrub Hill are converted from oil lamps to electric lamps.
30th May 1999	"CATHEDRALS EXPRESS" is renamed.
September 1999	CCTV installed at Shrub Hill. CCTV had also been installed at Foregate street station 6 months earlier.
11th Feb 2000	Water tower on depot taken down & cut up on site.
5th March 2000	First class 170 unit arrives at Worcester SH, for crew training (170517).
10th April 2000	First class 67 diesel loco to arrive at Worcester Shrub Hill 67005, on crew training Bristol/Bescot.
15th October 2000	Rail gala held at Shrub Hill station to mark the station's 150th anniversary.

Abbreviations

B & G	Birmingham & Gloucester
BRCW	Birmingham Railway Carriage & Wagon Co.
DMU	Diesel Multiple Unit
GWR	Great Western Railway
HST	High Speed Train (class 43)
OWWR	Oxford, Wolverhampton & Worcester Railway
LMS	London & Midland & Scottish
MAS	Multiple Aspect Signalling
LNER	London & North Eastern Railway
T.O.P.S	British Rail computer system (Total Operation Systems)
WD	War Department
WR	Western Region

Thanks

This book could not have been written without the help of the following:-

David Badham, Albert Baylis, Jim Beechey, Brent Carter, Jack Carter, Ian Catling, Central Trains, John Connolly,County Record Office, Michael Clemens, Edward Clissold, Martin Edgeworth, First Great Western, Alan Gibson, Roy Godfrey, Liz Godfrey, Dave Gommersoll, Steve Green, Howard Griffiths, Mike Grundy, Brian Harris, Denise Johnson, Trevor Lettice, The late Bruce Maher, Modern Railways, Harold Newnes, Tina Oliver, Julian Palfrey, David Paggett, John Pardoe, J.A Peden, Mrs Ruth Poole, Ray Pingrif, Rail Railway Magazine, Railtrack, John Ranford, Jack Saunders, Bob Sim, Bill Smith, Roger Thomas, Thames Trains, Fred Tyler, John Webster, Worcester Locomotive Society, Worcester Evening News, Worcester 150 committee, All Staff at Worcester Shrub Hill & Foregate Street Station.

As much information was put into this book as possible, however due to pressure on space in this book not everything could go in, & we are sure that there is much more that we have missed. If you know of something which has been missed, or something in this book which is wrong please contact us.

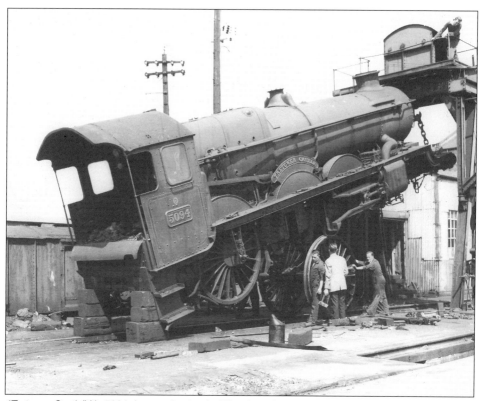

"Tretower Castle" No.5094, is seen having its Wheels replaced at Worcester Works in October 1961, this was one of the last times this operation was carry out at Worcester.

(Photo: Courtesy of the late Bruce Maher)